WHAT'S SO AMAZING ABOUT GRACE?

STUDY GUIDE

Also by Philip Yancey

The Jesus I Never Knew
What's So Amazing About Grace?
Where Is God When It Hurts?
Disappointment with God
The Student Bible, NIV (with Tim Stafford)
Church: Why Bother?
Discovering God
Finding God in Unexpected Places
The Jesus I Never Knew Study Guide (with Brenda Quinn)
The Jesus I Never Knew Study Guide video curriculum

Books by Dr. Paul Brand and Philip Yancey

Fearfully and Wonderfully Made
In His Image
The Gift of Pain

PHILIP YANCEY

with Brenda Quinn

WHAT'S SO AMAZING ABOUT GRACE?

STUDY GUIDE

ZondervanPublishingHouse

Grand Rapids, Michigan

A Division of HarperCollinsPublishers

What's So Amazing About Grace? Study Guide
Copyright © 1998 by Philip D. Yancey

Requests for information should be addressed to:

 ZondervanPublishingHouse
Grand Rapids, Michigan 49530

ISBN: 0-310-21904-3

Interior design by Sherri Hoffman

Printed in the United States of America

99 00 01 02 03 04 /❖ DC/ 10 9

Contents

Using This Study Guide

Little did I know what I was getting into when I began writing a book on the word *grace*. I chose the topic out of my concern that some of us in the U.S. church have lost our way and that we stand in danger of losing our most important contribution to the world. As I began my research, I came to see that grace underlies the gospel. Far from being some abstract theological doctrine, grace affects us in very practical ways: in family feuds, marital spats, even international crises.

I truly believe that the future of the church depends on how we master the art of "dispensing grace." Other groups—the Nation of Islam or the Pharisees, for example—excel at morality. Jesus taught us one great distinctive, that of grace, which has its own slow but steady power to change the world.

Thousands of people have bought and used the study guide for my last book, *The Jesus I Never Knew*, and we have produced this study guide partly in response to their encouragement. *What's So Amazing About Grace?* takes the principles I learned from Jesus and applies them in real-life, contemporary situations. Grace is not just about what happened two thousand years ago. It affects how we treat illegal aliens and former enemies, as well as outspoken pro-choice activists or other groups we might disagree with. It concerns what happens today, between you and your father or your unjust employer or the cranky neighbor down the street.

You can use this study guide either alone or in a group. If you use it individually, you should find that the questions build a bridge between my exploration of grace and your own. You may want to buy a blank notebook or personal journal (many bookstores sell these) in which to record your responses. Use this guide not as you would a textbook, feeling obligated to consider every question and fill in every blank, but rather as a series of suggestions. Linger over questions that arouse something inside you. Skip questions that don't seem to speak to your heart, and ignore those activities we've included that are designed for a group. You may find that adding just one person to your study—a spouse or a close friend, perhaps—makes it much more meaningful.

I have filled this book with stories because I believe that is the best way to comprehend grace. I hope they become springboards for your own stories, and that's why I encourage you to use this guide in a small group if possible. A small group is an ideal place to share stories of grace and ungrace. At its core, *grace* is a relationship word.

The experts I most respect on group interactions and soul-searching questions are the folks who produce the Serendipity House products, including *The Serendipity Bible.* For several decades they have been leading small groups and training other leaders, and I am thrilled again to have one of their former employees, Brenda Quinn, working with me on this study guide. Just as she did with the study guide for *The Jesus I Never Knew,* Brenda has taken my personal spiritual journey and adapted it into a form that others can use for their own journeys.

Advice for Small Groups

Ideally, a small group should not exceed twelve or at most fifteen members. Anything larger than that, and you'll likely find yourself reverting to a teacher-student structure in which the group leader dominates the discussion. Often, as you'll see, we encourage you to break into even smaller groups of four to six. Sometimes the best sharing takes place in these smaller groups, which some people find less intimidating.

We recommend choosing a leader in advance of each week's meeting (it need not be the same leader every week). This study guide recommends certain group activities, and each session includes far more content than most groups can cover in a single session. A good leader can scout these questions and activities in advance, deciding which seem most pertinent to the needs of your group. The more willing the leader is to open up and share from his or her life, the more willing the group members will be, so if you are the leader, take the role seriously. Think and pray about the group throughout the week before each meeting.

The study guide works best, of course, if everyone in the group has read the book we're studying, *What's So Amazing About Grace?* We follow its content chapter by chapter, sometimes combining two or three successive chapters in a session. Yet we also realize that in a busy world some people, no matter how well-intentioned, do not get around to reading material in advance. Others read it so far in advance that by the time the meeting rolls around, they can barely remember the content. For this reason we begin each session with a highly condensed summary of the chapter or chapters to be discussed. Some groups may choose to read this summary aloud to set the tone for the discussion to follow.

Using Music and Movies About Grace

As I said earlier, my book is filled with stories because I believe that is the best way to understand grace. For similar reasons we've included music in this study guide. Like stories, music has a powerful way of reaching the heart. Music penetrates and moves us in a way discussion alone cannot do. We have included a few music options at the end of each session and encourage you to incorporate music into your prayer time at the end of each meeting. You'll find that the suggested music is quite diverse from week to week, ranging from classical to contemporary Christian to gospel to country. You may choose to locate the recordings we've suggested, or you may prefer to use the hymns or praise songs we give as alternatives. You may also know of other appropriate music to use. This time can be one more way of letting God speak to individuals and to your group.

Occasionally we suggest gathering the group between meetings to view a film that tells a story of grace. This is optional, and individuals may want to watch the movies on their own if the group is unable to get together. One film I discuss in the book is a documentary on John Newton's famous hymn, *Amazing Grace with Bill Moyers.* The film tells the story of the hymn and features the Boys Choir of Harlem, Johnny Cash, Judy Collins, and many others. The film might be a good introductory activity for the group as your study begins. Or you may want to show just a clip from the film at the last session, as suggested there. Some large video rental stores have the film available to rent. You can purchase it for $24.95 through Gateway Films/Vision Video (1-800-523-0226).

Leading Group Discussion

Although group study is highly valuable, it carries challenges— the same challenges experienced in the church, on a smaller and sometimes more intense scale. But don't let these challenges keep you from the bonding and growth achieved through life together. Enter with realistic expectations, knowing that as in all relationships, there will be irritations, times when you don't feel like being together, people you don't particularly like, and probably even a period of disillusionment with the group. This is normal, just as it is normal in every family and in every friendship. Press on together. Most often you will find that God will bless individuals and group relationships in deep and lasting ways that far outweigh the difficult times you encounter.

As you meet together, keep the discussion moving. Don't be afraid of short silences, especially at first when members are moving deeper into a topic. But don't let the discussion die, either. During a pause you may ask, "Does anyone have thoughts on this issue?" If silence continues or discussion remains minimal, don't be afraid to admit it: "Why don't we feel like talking about this today?"

The discussion may be less than provocative in other ways. It may start to snowball, with everyone agreeing with each other. In such cases you may need to play "devil's advocate" and argue the other side to force people to really think. At other times a few vocal people may dominate the discussion. You can counteract this by calling on others who have something to say, by watching especially for timid members who are afraid to jump in, and by even taking the talkative ones aside after the meeting and asking them to share the time a little better.

Here are some suggestions for communicating throughout the discussion.

- When you believe that the speaker is making assumptions: "Why do you believe that? What have you experienced that makes you think so?"
- When you feel yourself becoming angry or uncomfortable: "Is anyone else feeling uneasy about this?" Don't feel a need for all to come to agreement, or remain silent when you disagree with a statement. Further discussion will air feelings and prevent hidden emotions from erupting later in more destructive ways.
- When the main focus has been lost or an interesting point has been dropped amid further discussion: "Let's go back to the original question." "Could we go back to what was said earlier about _____?" "Could we talk a little more about _____?"
- When you sense the need to clarify: "Do you mean that a Christian should hate an immoral person or, rather, that we should hate immoral things people do?"
- When you think there is more to what someone is saying: "Do you know why you feel this way?" "When did you first begin to feel this way?"
- When someone is obviously passionate about a viewpoint: Affirm their right to feel strongly and assure them that they've been understood by summarizing back to them what they've said before you agree or disagree ("You really feel strongly about this. You're saying that . . .").
- When someone is sharing something difficult and personal: "I've felt that way, too. I can understand." "I haven't

experienced that, so I appreciate your helping me to understand better what it was like."

Lastly—this probably goes without saying—be sensitive and respectful. Realize that many issues discussed in this study will be difficult. They will challenge some people's long-held assumptions and practices. It takes time to process new ideas, especially those related to the Bible, our way of life, and our relationships with God and others. Don't feel a need to find all the answers in an hour or two. Most of us will continue thinking about these issues for the rest of our lives.

A Final Word

I encourage you not to feel hemmed in by the structure we've set out in this study guide. Although the book contains twenty chapters, we've divided the content into fourteen sessions for this study guide, occasionally combining chapters. Churches who follow a twelve- or thirteen-week cycle of study will need to make some adjustments. And if your group gets excited about the content of one session, by all means don't squelch the interest and slavishly turn to a new topic the next week. Follow up on the discussion.

The same principle applies to individual questions. Don't cut off a stimulating discussion out of some obligation to plow through every single question. Conversely, if your group bogs down, move on until you find something that seems to generate interest. Remember, this small group study is not a school assignment, with a goal of finishing all the material. Our goal is for you to encounter God and his grace, and that may happen in unpredictable, unplanned ways. Allow room for God's Spirit to work in your group.

And by all means, have fun! You may find that the topic of grace becomes especially challenging at times. But let yourself move past the difficulties of grace to the great joy that belongs to us because of our surprising, grace-filled God.

The Last Best Word

Chapter 1

❧

As a writer, I play with words all day long. I toy with them, listen for their overtones, crack them open, and try to stuff my thoughts inside. I've found that words tend to spoil over the years, like old meat. Their meaning rots away.

Perhaps I keep circling back to *grace* because it is one grand theological word that has not spoiled. I call it "the last best word" because every English usage I can find retains some of the glory of the original. Like a vast aquifer, the word underlies our proud civilization, reminding us that good things come not from our own efforts, rather by the grace of God. Even now, taproots still stretch toward grace as seen in words such as *grateful, gratified, congratulated, gracious, gratuity, ingrate, disgrace,* and my favorite, *persona non grata.*

The many uses of the word in English convince me that *grace* is indeed amazing—truly our last best word. It contains the essence of the gospel as a drop of water can contain the image of the sun. The world thirsts for grace in ways it does not even recognize; little wonder the hymn "Amazing Grace" edged its way onto the Top Ten charts two hundred years after composition. For a society that seems adrift, without moorings, I know of no better place to drop an anchor of faith.

Oddly, I sometimes find a shortage of grace within the church, an institution founded to proclaim, in Paul's phrase, "the gospel of God's grace." Trace the roots of *grace,* or *charis* in Greek, and you will find a verb that means "I rejoice, I am glad." In my experience, rejoicing and gladness are not the first images that come to mind when people think of the church. They think of holier-than-thous. They think of church as a place to go after you have cleaned up your act, not before. They think of morality, not grace.

As I look back on my own pilgrimage, marked by wanderings, detours, and dead ends, I see now that what pulled me along was my search for grace. I rejected the church for a time because I found so little grace there. I returned because I found grace nowhere else.

I have barely tasted of grace myself, have rendered less than I have received, and am in no wise an "expert" on grace. These are, in fact, the very reasons that impel me to write. I want to know more, to understand more, to experience more grace. I dare not— and the danger is very real—write an ungracious book about grace. Accept then, here at the beginning, that I write as a pilgrim qualified only by my craving for grace.

The Music of Grace in God's Word

Read together the following passage from the Bible.

John 8:1–11

The Harmony of Grace Around Me and Within
(20 Minutes)

If you are in a larger group, break into groups of four to six for this discussion time. Introduce yourselves to each other. Tell the others briefly about yourself. Are you single? Married? Do you have children? Do you work outside the home?

1. What comes to mind when you hear the word *grace*? Be honest. We're all coming at grace from different places.

   - A religious word that draws a blank
   - A word that makes me uncomfortable
   - A word that gives me hope
   - The story of my life
   - A yearning I feel inside
   - Other: _____

2. Why did you decide to take part in this study? As you tell the others, focus on your own life and what you hope to gain.

3. Read together the story about the prostitute on page 11 in the book. Try to put yourself in the shoes of the one sitting with the woman and hearing her story. What would have been your initial reaction? What would you have said to her?

4. Think about the story of the prostitute alongside the story of the woman caught in adultery in John 8. "Church!" the prostitute cried. "Why would I ever go there? I was already feeling terrible about myself. They'd just make me feel worse." It seems the prostitute was merely reflecting what has been a reality with religious people for millennia.

   Read verses 3–5 from John 8 again. If you need a refresher on God's Law given through Moses, look at Leviticus 20:10 and Deuteronomy 22:22. Who else should have been punished, according to God's Law?

What new attitude toward the law does God show through the person of Jesus? See verse 7.

Turn again to the modern-day story of the prostitute. We are no longer living in Old Testament days but in Jesus' days. We cannot, and must not, forget God's desire for our holiness. But neither can we stop there. God gave us Jesus to express his deep love, even for people who don't deserve him. How then should our response to the prostitute differ from the Pharisees' response to the adulterous woman?

What might it look like if an individual or a church responded with grace to the prostitute's plea for help?

Optional: If you have time, read the story about another prostitute and a party Tony Campolo threw. The story is printed at the end of this session, in the "Background Music of Grace This Week" section. If you don't have time to read it now, you can read it on your own this week.

5. Read the quote by David Seamands on page 15 in the book. Do you agree with Seamands? Can you think of an example in your own life that supports his statement? Share as you feel comfortable.

6. As I look back on my own pilgrimage, marked by wanderings, detours, and dead ends, I see now that what pulled me along was my search for grace. I rejected the church for a time because I found so little grace there. I returned because I found grace nowhere else.

What has your search for grace been like?

Do you have any prayer needs you would like to share with this group?

God's Song of Grace to Me
(10–15 Minutes)

This last section of each study will give you a few minutes to sit quietly with God and meditate on grace. First you will listen to or sing a song that puts grace to music. You have read and heard stories of grace. Now music, like story, will help us to take grace inside, to connect our minds with our hearts. During these minutes music will help you open yourself to God's presence. Close your eyes as you listen or as you sing. Ask God to speak through the words and move your soul through the music.

Then sit in silence for several minutes in the presence of God as a corporate body. You may not be accustomed to sharing in quiet time together, but give it a try. As you become comfortable, you'll find it a rich experience. If you'd like, bring a notebook or blank book to use as a journal. Or write your thoughts in the space provided in this study guide. You may want to pray or meditate on Scripture. You'll find a prayer below. You can add on to the prayer in the space provided or in your journal. If you are using this guide on your own, use music as you are able, or simply spend the time in prayer, meditation, and journaling.

Grace Notes

Listen together to the song "Amazing Grace." A powerful gospel version of the song can be found on the CD or cassette titled *Love Brought Me Back* by Helen Baylor (Word, 1996). If you can't obtain Baylor's version, use another version of the song available to you. Or distribute the words and sing with a guitar, piano, or *a capella*.

———

God, I have a lot to learn about grace, and a lot to learn about you. I know I've seen your grace in my life, more than once. When I think about the ways you've graced me, I fall silent. I'm thinking of salvation, yes, and of all those times I deserved punishment and got forgiveness. Those times I deserved nothing and got something. Your grace hasn't been absent. But maybe it has become stagnant, stuck in pools inside me with too few outlets. Your notes of grace ring loud and true. Now help me to make the music....

Joining in the Song of Grace

- Keep an ear out this week for uses of the word *grace* and for variations of this word. Make a mental note when you hear the word being used. What meaning is intended? Does the word still carry its original meaning? Does it still impact people deeply?
- Consider two or three struggles you are experiencing right now. Think about these in relation to the quote by David Seamands on page 15 in the book. Do your struggles have

anything to do with your own inabilities to accept or to live out God's grace? Make this a matter of prayer.

• Consider gathering together as a group sometime before the next group meeting to watch the movie *Babette's Feast*. Or watch the movie on your own. This film is available at many video rental stores. The story appears in chapter 2, and we will be discussing it at the next meeting.

Background Music of Grace This Week
(Optional)

You can integrate this study into your life throughout the week by using the following Bible passages and story in your quiet moments. Reflect on these readings as your time allows.

Day 1: Nehemiah 9:16–18; Proverbs 3:34; Jonah 2:6–9
Day 2: John 1:1–18
Day 3: Acts 4:32–34; Acts 11:19–24
Day 4: Romans 3:21–31
Day 5: 2 Corinthians 5:16–6:2

Tony Campolo tells about being invited to speak in Honolulu one time and having trouble getting his body to adjust to the ten-hour time shift from his home in Philadelphia. He wound up wide-awake at three o'clock in the morning drinking coffee in an all-night diner. Presently the door opened, and in came about eight women laughing and talking loudly. Campolo soon deduced that they were streetwalkers finished with their evening's work and relaxing before going home to sleep. One, named Agnes, mentioned to her friend that the next day would be her thirty-ninth birthday.

After the group left, Campolo got a bright idea. He said to the gruff proprietor behind the counter, "Did you hear that one woman say tomorrow was her birthday? Whaddya say we throw her a party? I'll come back tomorrow night with some decorations, and let's surprise her with a cake and everything!"

The man's wife came out of the kitchen. Both of them said, "That is a wonderful idea. Let's do it."

Twenty-four hours later the little diner was decorated with streamers and balloons. A festive sign was taped to the mirror. The couple had put the word out on the street, and a large assortment of night people were gathered. When the prostitutes came in for their usual coffee, the shout went up: "Happy birthday, Agnes!"

The woman stood speechless as the singing began. Tears started to roll down her cheeks. Nobody had showed her genuine kindness in years. The owner brought out a birthday cake with candles. Agnes was in such shock that she had to be reminded to blow them out.

She paused again. "Well, cut the cake, Agnes!" the proprietor said.

She finally found words. In a whisper she said, "Please . . . I just . . . I just want to keep the cake. I'll take it to my apartment down the street . . . just for a couple of days. Please let me keep the cake."

No one knew how to respond, but no one could think of a reason to refuse her request. So out the door she fled, holding the cake as if it were the Holy Grail.

An awkward silence filled the room. Campolo finally broke in with a bold suggestion: "I have another idea—why don't we pray?" Without hesitation he began to voice a prayer for Agnes, that God would bless her on her birthday, that God would bring peace into her life and save her from all that troubled her . . .

At the amen, the diner owner said, "Hey—you didn't tell me you were a preacher. What kind of church do you preach at?"

Campolo thought a moment, cocked his head sideways, and then answered with a grin, "I preach at the kind of church that throws birthday parties for whores at three-thirty in the morning!"

What happened next was the most poignant moment of all. The man squinted at Campolo and announced, "No . . . no, you don't. There is no church like that. I would join a church like that."[1]

Week Two

What Grace Is and Isn't

Chapters 2–3

Igrew up in a church that drew sharp lines between "the age of Law" and "the age of Grace." While ignoring most moral prohibitions from the Old Testament, we had our own pecking order rivaling the Orthodox Jews'. At the top were smoking and drinking. Movies ranked just below these vices, with many church members refusing even to attend *The Sound of Music*. Rock music, then in its infancy, was likewise regarded as an abomination, quite possibly demonic in origin.

Other proscriptions—wearing makeup and jewelry, reading the Sunday paper, playing or watching sports on Sunday, mixed swimming, skirt length for girls, hair length for boys—were heeded or not heeded depending on a person's level of spirituality. I grew up with the strong impression that a person became spiritual by attending to these gray-area rules. For the life of me, I could not figure out much difference between the dispensations of Law and Grace.

Mark Twain used to talk about people who were "good in the worst sense of the word," a phrase that, for many, captures the reputation of Christians today. Recently I have been asking a question of strangers—for example, seatmates on an airplane—when I strike up a conversation. "When I say the words 'evangelical Christian' what comes to mind?" In reply, mostly I hear political descriptions: of strident pro-life activists, or gay-rights opponents, or proposals for censoring the Internet. I hear references to the Moral Majority, an organization disbanded years ago. Not once—*not once*—have I heard a description redolent of grace. Apparently that is not the aroma Christians give off in the world.

I have been picking on Christians because I am one, and see no reason to pretend we are better than we are. I fight the tentacular grip of ungrace in my own life. Although I may not perpetuate the strictness of my upbringing, I battle daily against pride, judgmentalism, and a feeling that I must somehow earn God's approval. By instinct I feel I must *do something* in order to be accepted. Grace sounds a startling note of contradiction, of liberation, and every day I must pray anew for the ability to hear its message.

In truth, though, a virulent strain of ungrace shows up in all religions. Even the best humanists devise systems of ungrace to replace those rejected in religion. The military, corporations, schools, sports franchises, and every institution, it seems, run on ungrace and its insistence that we *earn* our way. Even cultural definitions of beauty communicate ungrace. We live in an atmosphere choked with the fumes of ungrace. Grace comes from outside, as a gift and not an achievement. How easily it vanishes from our dog-eat-dog, survival-of-the-fittest, look-out-for-number-one world.

Grace comes free of charge to people who do not deserve it and I am one of those people. I think back to who I was—resentful, wound tight with anger, a single hardened link in a long chain of ungrace learned from family and church. Now I am trying in my own small way to pipe the tune of grace. I do so because I know, more surely than I know anything, that any pang of healing or forgiveness or goodness I have ever felt comes solely from the grace of God. I yearn for the church to become a nourishing culture of that grace.

The Music of Grace in God's Word

Wait until you are instructed in the next section to read together the following passages from the Bible.

Mark 14:1–9
Mark 10:13–16

~

The Harmony of Grace Around Me and Within
(25 Minutes)

If you are in a larger group, break into groups of four to six for this discussion time. Introduce yourselves to each other if necessary. Tell the group about the most memorable "feast" you can recall. What food was served? Whom did you eat with?

1. *Optional:* If some in your group haven't read chapter 2 in the book, titled "Babette's Feast: A Story," have someone read the story aloud. This will take some extra time. Even if you have all read the story, you may want to review it together. It is found on pages 19–26.

   Have you seen this movie, or read the original version of the story by Isak Dinesen, of a woman named Babette who moves to Scandinavia after a civil war in France and takes up residence with two sisters heading a strict religious sect? Members of the sect live, and eat, very simply, believing this to be the biblical way. Babette wins a lottery and spends the entire large sum on an extravagant dinner for the sisters and their sect members. How does the story make you feel?

- Baffled that people could live the way this sect did year after year.
- Frustrated for the sect and the sisters, for needlessly forfeiting so much.
- Sorry for Babette.
- Uncomfortable—I see some of myself, and my church background, in the sisters.
- Touched—we all live ungrace-filled lives much of the time. This story is a good reminder that we really can do things to intentionally break out of this pattern.
- Other: _____

How do you think Babette felt after the feast? Did she regret blowing her fortune?

2. Read Mark 14:1–9. Think about the story of Babette and the story of the woman in Mark 14. What motivated each to do what she did? What motivated the sisters in Babette's story, and the dinner companions in Jesus' story, to react as they did?

Can you think of a time when, like Babette and like the woman with the perfume, you performed a senseless act or gave an extravagant gift? How did you feel doing it? What was the response?

Can you recall a time when someone did something like this for you? How did you feel receiving it?

3. On page 30 in the book I talk about the many rules that were a part of the church of my childhood. Did your church or community have similar rules when you grew up? What was your church environment like? If you did not grow up going to church, what was your community or family environment like? How did this affect you?

Review the piece by Erma Bombeck on page 32 in the book. Why would a churchgoer feel a child shouldn't smile in church? Read Mark 10:13–16. What was Jesus' attitude about children and about adults?

4. On page 31 in the book read the paragraph in which I talk about asking the question, "When I say the words 'evangelical Christian' what comes to mind?" If you were to ask that question of those you know who are not Christians, what do you think their response would be?

In a thoroughly secular culture, the church is more likely to show ungrace through a spirit of moral superiority or a fierce attitude toward opponents in the "culture wars." The church also communicates ungrace through its lack of unity (page 33 in the book).

Bill Hybels, author and pastor of Willow Creek Community Church, notes similar observations. He says,

> I sometimes strike up casual conversations with people who don't know what I do for a living. "I'm curious," I'll say. "Do you know any Christians? And if you do, what are they like?" ... Far more frequently than I wish to admit, people produce some unsettling answers. They'll say, "I know some Christians and, well, I'd have to describe them as sort of uptight and narrow. You know—really rigid types." Others will say, "They're sort of isolated. They keep to themselves. I don't know them well because they're in their own world." Other reports are worse: "I know some born-againers, and I've got to tell you, they really bother me. I feel like I'm being condemned every time I walk by them. They're just too self-righteous." Or, "They're so simplistic, rattling off trite Bible answers for every complex problem."[1]

Do you see any of these characteristics in yourself? (Don't spend a lot of time discussing this question, as we will be considering similar questions in future sessions.)

5. On page 36 in the book read the two paragraphs about Lewis Smedes. Smedes has identified three common sources of crippling shame: secular culture, graceless religion, and unaccepting parents. Have any of these been a factor in your life?

Now might be a good time for some introspection. Have you contributed toward anyone else's shame by reinforcing any of these sources? For example, have you communicated to others that they must look good, feel good, and make good? In associations with unbelievers, have you stressed the rules of Christianity more than the grace available? Have you made your child feel he or she will never quite meet your approval?

6. On pages 38–39 in the book I talk about some experiences of unexpected grace (in a store, on a mountain, and in Rome). Later, on pages 41–42, I tell of how grace came to me through music, nature, and romantic love. What have been the channels of grace in your life?

Do you have any prayer needs to express to the group?

God's Song of Grace to Me
(10–15 Minutes)

Listen to some music about grace together, and then spend some time in silence with God. You may want to reflect on the words from Bach's "O Sacred Head," printed below. Or you can spend the time in prayer. If you choose to write a prayer or take notes, you can use the space provided or write in your journal.

Grace Notes

Listen together to the chorale "O Sacred Head" from *St. Matthew Passion* by Johann Sebastian Bach. Many public libraries will have this CD available to borrow. Bach has long been acclaimed as one of the most gifted and committed Christian composers of all time. He was an outstanding singer and organist and played several other instruments. Bach possessed a deep personal faith in Christ. He considered all his music, both sacred and secular, to be for the glory of God, routinely initialing the letters "S.D.G." (*Soli Deo Gloria*—"To God alone, the glory") at the end of his compositions. Next to 2 Chronicles 5:13, which describes a temple worship service, Bach wrote in his biblical commentary, "Where there is devotional music, God is always at hand with his gracious presence."[2] *St. Matthew Passion* is the story of the Crucifixion, written for Good Friday. The chorale you will hear was sung by the congregation five times during the course of the five-hour service. As you listen, think of the grace that Jesus embodied as he gave his life for you, a sinner.

If you do not have access to a recording of this piece by Bach, find the words to "O Sacred Head, Now Wounded" in a hymnal. Sing together with a piano, guitar, or *a capella*.

O Sacred Head

O sacred head sore wounded
Defiled and put to scorn!
O Kingly Head surrounded
With mocking crown of thorn!
What sorrow mars Thy grandeur?
Can death Thy bloom deflower?
O countenance whose splendor
The hosts of heaven adore.
Thy beauty long desired,
Hath vanished from our sight.
Thy power is all expired,
And quenched the Light of Light.
Ah me! For whom Thou diest,
Hide not so far Thy grace;
Show me, O Love most highest,
The brightness of Thy face.

Johann Sebastian Bach

Joining in the Song of Grace

- This week surprise someone in your life with an unexpected act of grace. Do something that may even be uncharacteristic of you.
- This week think about the things you do that may be done to win God's, or the church's, approval. Don't immediately stop doing them, but begin praying about your motives and ask for God's help in gaining his perspective on how you should live.
- Consider gathering the group together before the next meeting to watch the movie *Amadeus*, about Wolfgang Amadeus Mozart. If the group can't get together, consider watching the movie on your own in preparation for next week's study. The theme of grace pervades this movie on several levels. The movie is available at most video rental stores.

Background Music of Grace This Week
(Optional)

Read the following Bible passages this week in your quiet moments. Reflect on these readings as your time allows.

Day 1: Psalm 145
Day 2: Hosea 3:1–4:6
Day 3: Hosea 11:1–11
Day 4: Matthew 5:13–16
Day 5: Matthew 5:43–6:4

Week Three

Grace in the Bible

Chapters 4–5

~

During a British conference on comparative religions, experts from around the world debated what, if any, belief was unique to the Christian faith. They began eliminating possibilities. Incarnation? Resurrection? No—other religions had accounts of these. The debate went on for some time until C. S. Lewis wandered into the room. "What's the rumpus about?" he asked, and heard in reply that his colleagues were discussing Christianity's unique contribution among world religions. Lewis responded, "Oh, that's easy. It's grace."

After some discussion, the conferees had to agree. The notion of God's love coming to us free of charge, no strings attached, seems to go against every instinct of humanity. The Buddhist eight-fold path, the Hindu doctrine of *karma,* the Jewish covenant, and Muslim code of law—each of these offers a way to earn approval. Only Christianity dares to make God's love unconditional.

Aware of our inbuilt resistance to grace, Jesus talked about it often. Yet he never analyzed or defined grace, and almost never used the word. Instead, he communicated grace through stories we know as parables. When I study the parables, I come away with a very strange message indeed. Obviously, Jesus did not give the parables to teach us how to live. He gave them, I believe, to correct our notions about who God is and who God loves.

The gospel is not at all what we would come up with on our own. I, for one, would expect to honor the virtuous over the profligate. I would expect to have to clean up my act before even applying for an audience with a Holy God. But Jesus told of God ignoring a fancy religious teacher and turning instead to an ordinary sinner who pleads, "God, have mercy." Throughout the Bible, in fact, God shows a marked preference for "real" people over "good" people. In Jesus' own words, "There will be more rejoicing in heaven over one sinner who repents than over ninety-nine righteous persons who do not need to repent."

Ask people what they must do to get to heaven and most reply, "Be good." Jesus' stories contradict that answer. All we must do is cry, "Help!" God welcomes home anyone who will have him and, in fact, has made the first move already.

In the Old Testament stories of Jacob, Samson, David, and Solomon, the scandal of grace rumbles under the surface. Finally, in Jesus' parables, it bursts forth in a dramatic upheaval to reshape the moral landscape.

Jesus' parable of the workers and their grossly unfair paychecks confronts this scandal head-on. In a contemporary Jewish version of this story, the workers hired late in the afternoon work so hard that the employer, impressed, decides to award them a full day's wages. Not so in Jesus' version, which notes that the last crop of workers have been idly standing around in the marketplace, something only lazy, shiftless workers would do during harvest season. Moreover, these laggards do nothing to distinguish themselves, and the other workers are shocked by the pay they receive. What employer in his right mind would pay the same amount for one hour's work as for twelve!

Jesus' story makes no economic sense, and that was his intent. He was giving us a parable about grace, which cannot be calculated like a day's wages. We receive grace as a gift from God, not as something we toil to earn.

Significantly, many Christians who study this parable identify with the employees who put in a full day's work, rather than the add-ons at the end of the day. We like to think of ourselves as responsible workers, and the employer's strange behavior baffles us as it did the original hearers. We risk missing the story's point: that God dispenses gifts, not wages. None of us gets paid according to merit, for none of us comes close to satisfying God's requirements for a perfect life. If paid on the basis of fairness, we would all end up in hell.

I grew up with the image of a mathematical God who weighed my good and bad deeds on a set of scales and always found me wanting. Somehow I missed the God of the Gospels, a God of mercy and generosity who keeps finding ways to shatter the relentless laws of ungrace. God tears up the mathematical tables and introduces the new math of *grace,* the most surprising, twisting, unexpected-ending word in the English language.

God is "the God of all grace," in the apostle Peter's words. And grace means there is nothing I can do to make God love me more, and nothing I can do to make God love me less. It means that I, even I who deserve the opposite, am invited to take my place at the table in God's family.

The Music of Grace in God's Word

Wait until you are instructed in the next section to look together at the following passages from the Bible.

Matthew 18:21–35
Luke 14:12–24
Luke 15:11–32
Matthew 20:1–16

The Harmony of Grace Around Me and Within
(25 Minutes)

If you are in a larger group, break into groups of four to six for this discussion time. Introduce yourselves to each other if necessary. Have you ever won something randomly, maybe a door prize, a drawing, or some other unexpected gift? What did you win? How did you feel?

[Leader: You may find it meaningful to read aloud one or two of the modern-day parables discussed in the following questions. You probably won't have time to get through each of questions 1–4, especially if you choose to read aloud. Choose a couple of the questions, or choose to answer the questions without reading the parables aloud.]

1. Look at the modern-day parable about the entrepreneur in Los Angeles on pages 47–48 in the book.

   How likely do you think this story is to happen today? How many individuals today would offer a large sum of money for a new enterprise, only to see the venture fail and the money disappear without requiring anything in return from the debtor? Have you ever received a significant gift of money, with no strings attached? Or been released from a debt you owed? Share only as you feel comfortable. How did this gift or removal of debt make you feel? How significant was this gift in your life?

Look at the story in Matthew 18:21–35. Why would the servant turn around, after receiving such mercy, and treat a fellow servant so unmercifully?

2. Look at the modern-day parable about the woman in Boston who gave a banquet for the homeless after her wedding was canceled. This parable is on pages 48–49 in the book.

How do you think the hotel staff felt serving addicts and bag ladies on that banquet evening? Do you think most people have something in them, deep down, that senses the rightness of grace, despite its rareness in our world?

Look at the story of the wedding banquet Jesus described in Luke 14:16–24. How do you think the master felt after the banquet—glad for hosting those who aren't used to feasting, or begrudging toward those who would never repay him? How do you feel when you give to someone who probably won't reciprocate? Do your feelings depend on how needy the other person is?

3. Look at the modern-day parable about the girl from Tra-
verse City, Michigan, on pages 49–51 in the book.

Do you think most fathers today would respond in the
way this girl's father did, inviting the relatives to welcome
home a runaway daughter who had been involved in
prostitution? Would most families throw a party upon
her return, the way this family did? Are there any "prodi-
gals" in your extended family? How are they treated?

Look at the story of the prodigal son in Luke 15:11–32.
Do you usually relate more to the older son or the prodigal
son? Where do you think God wants you to see yourself?

4. Read together the modern-day parable about the vagrant
in Manhattan on page 46 in the book. Now review the
parable about the workers in the field in Matthew 20:1–
16. And now think about some Old Testament stories if
you know them: the story of Jacob, the conniver who was
God's chosen over his dutiful brother Esau; the story of
the carousing Samson, who received supernatural powers
of strength; the story of David, a shepherd boy who
became Israel's king. There is a saying, "Life isn't fair."
More precisely, it seems God isn't fair. Can you think of

something good in your life you have received that wasn't really fair?

5. Reflect: From nursery school onward we are taught how to succeed in the world of ungrace. Work hard for what you earn. The early bird gets the worm. No pain, no gain. There is no such thing as a free lunch. Demand your rights. Get what you pay for. I know these rules well because I live by them. I work for what I earn; I like to win; I insist on my rights. I want fairness. I want people to get what they deserve—nothing more, nothing less.

Yet if I care to listen, I hear a loud whisper from the gospel that I did not get what I deserved. I deserved punishment and got forgiveness. I deserved wrath and got love. I deserved debtor's prison and got instead a clean credit history. I deserved stern lectures and crawl-on-your-knees repentance; I got a banquet—Babette's feast—spread for me.

6. Review the story of the prophet Hosea, which I talk about on pages 65–66 in the book. It's not hard to imagine today how Hosea would be viewed by his society upon taking his unfaithful wife back. He would probably be considered codependent, dysfunctional, naïve. Yet Hosea accurately reflects God and his bride, the church. God's emotions and his actions mirror those of Hosea in dealing with the people he loves. God allows himself to endure great humiliation, only to come back for more. At the heart of the gospel is a God who deliberately surrenders to the wild, irresistible power of love.

If our God acts out his love for us in such a way, how does that make you feel about the mistakes you've made in the past and God's attitude toward you right now?

Do you have any prayer needs to share with the group?

God's Song of Grace to Me
(10–15 Minutes)

Listen together to some music that heralds God's grace. Close your eyes and let the music speak to you of God as you sit in his presence. Then sit in silence for several minutes, enjoying these moments with God as a corporate body. You can reflect on the words of the music or perhaps on the words about grace printed at the end of this section. You may want to write in your journal or in the space provided, expressing a prayer or your reflections on today's study.

Grace Notes

Listen together to a piece from Mozart's *Requiem*, titled "Kyrie." The words translate into English, "Lord, have mercy upon us. Christ, have mercy upon us. Lord, have mercy upon us."

Wolfgang Amadeus Mozart was a child prodigy and a virtual genius as a composer. Recent portrayals of Mozart don't accurately tell of his spiritual life, however. In a letter to his father Mozart wrote, "Papa must not worry, for God is ever before my eyes. I realize His omnipotence and I fear His anger; but I also recognize His love, His compassion, and His tenderness towards His creatures. He will never forsake His own." Mozart's generous and compassionate spirit once prompted him to help a beggar in the streets of Vienna. Having no money to offer, he brought the man into a coffeehouse and quickly wrote an entire minuet and trio, wrote a letter to his publisher, and sent them with the beggar. The man received five guineas in return.

Mozart wrote his last work, *Requiem,* on his deathbed at age thirty-five. His treatment of centuries-old Latin text expresses his strong faith in "The Lamb of God, who takes away the sin of the world." Mozart felt death was imminent as he wrote, and expressed to his wife that he was writing *Requiem* for himself.[1] These words from *Requiem* can be our confident prayer: "Remember, merciful Jesu, That I am the cause of your journey."

Many public libraries will have Mozart's *Requiem* available to borrow. If you do not have access to Mozart or would prefer an alternate piece of music, obtain the CD or cassette by Point of Grace titled *The Whole Truth* (Word, 1995). Listen together to the song "The Great Divide."

Or find in a hymnal the song "The Old Rugged Cross." Sing together with a piano, guitar, or *a capella.*

Joining in the Song of Grace

- This week carry with you the words "I am the one Jesus loves." Fasten them to your bathroom mirror, the kitchen sink, or your car dashboard if this will help to keep the words running through your mind. Let these words transform your week.
- Consider reading the book *The Return of the Prodigal Son* by Henri Nouwen. The author puts himself in the place of each person in the parable of the prodigal son and reflects on how we can identify with each character.

• This week talk about grace with a few family members, friends, or acquaintances. Ask them how they feel about the following definition of grace: Grace means there is nothing we can do to make God love us more, and nothing we can do to make God love us less.

Background Music of Grace This Week
(Optional)

Use the following Bible passages in your quiet moments this week as you reflect on God's grace. Use these readings as your time allows.

Day 1: Matthew 18:21–35
Day 2: Luke 14:12–24
Day 3: Luke 15:11–32
Day 4: Matthew 20:1–16
Day 5: Romans 3:21–31; Isaiah 55

Forgiveness: An Unnatural Act

Chapters 6–7

Ungrace plays like the background static of life for families, nations, and institutions. It is, sadly, our natural human state. Ungrace does its work quietly and lethally, like a poisonous, undetectable gas. A father dies unforgiven. A mother who once carried a child in her own body does not speak to that child for half its life. The toxin steals on, from generation to generation.

Ungrace causes cracks to fissure open between mother and daughter, father and son, brother and sister, between scientists, and prisoners, and tribes, and races. Left alone, cracks widen, and for the resulting chasms of ungrace there is only one remedy: the frail rope-bridge of forgiveness.

In the heat of an argument my wife came up with an acute theological formulation. We were discussing my shortcomings in a rather spirited way when she said, "I think it's pretty amazing that I forgive you for some of the dastardly things you've done!"

Since I'm writing about forgiveness, not sin, I will omit the juicy details of those dastardly things. What struck me about her comment, rather, was its sharp insight into the nature of forgiveness. It is no sweet platonic ideal to be dispersed in the world like air-freshener sprayed from a can. Forgiveness is achingly difficult.

Forgiveness is an unnatural act—my wife expressed this truth as if by instinct. The very taste of forgiveness seems somehow wrong. Even when we have committed a wrong, we want to earn our way back into the injured party's good graces. We prefer to crawl on our knees, to wallow, to do penance, to kill a lamb—and religion often obliges us.

Yet Jesus instructed us to "Forgive us our trespasses, as we forgive those who trespass against us." At the center of the Lord's Prayer, which Jesus taught us to recite, lurks the unnatural act of forgiveness. Jesus hinged God's forgiveness on our willingness to forgive unjust acts.

It is one thing to get caught up in a cycle of ungrace with a spouse or business partner, and another thing entirely to get caught in such a cycle with Almighty God. Yet the Lord's Prayer pulls those two together: As we can allow ourselves to let go, to break the cycle, to start over, God can allow himself to let go, break the cycle, start over.

Theologically, the Gospels give a straightforward answer to why God asks us to forgive: because that is what God is like. When Jesus first gave the command, "Love your enemies," he added this rationale: " . . . that you may be sons of your Father in heaven. He causes his sun to rise on the evil and the good, and sends rain on the righteous and the unrighteous."

The gospel of grace begins and ends with forgiveness. And people write songs with titles like "Amazing Grace" for one reason: grace is the only force in the universe powerful enough to break the chains that enslave generations. Grace alone melts ungrace.

God shattered the inexorable law of sin and retribution by invading earth, absorbing the worst we had to offer, crucifixion, and then fashioning from that cruel deed the remedy for the human condition. Calvary broke up the logjam between justice and forgiveness. By accepting onto his innocent self all the severe demands of justice, Jesus broke forever the chain of ungrace.

One day I discovered this admonition from the apostle Paul tucked in among many other admonitions in Romans 12. Hate evil, Be joyful, Live in harmony, Do not be conceited—the list goes on and on. Then appears this verse, "Do not take revenge, my friends, but leave room for God's wrath, for it is written: 'It is mine to avenge; I will repay,' says the Lord."

At last I understood: In the final analysis, forgiveness is an act of faith. By forgiving another, I am trusting that God is a better justice-maker than I am. By forgiving, I release my own right to get even and leave all issues of fairness for God to work out. I leave in God's hands the scales that must balance justice and mercy.

I never find forgiveness easy, and rarely do I find it completely satisfying. Nagging injustices remain, and the wounds still cause pain. I have to approach God again and again, yielding to him the residue of what I thought I had committed to him long ago. I do so because the Gospels make clear the connection: God forgives my debts as I forgive my debtors. The reverse is also true: Only by living in the stream of God's grace will I find the strength to respond with grace toward others.

The Music of Grace in God's Word

Read together the following passage from the Bible.

Genesis 37:12–28

Later you will read more of this story in Genesis 42:1–8, 18–26; 43:26–31; 45:1–11.

~

The Harmony of Grace Around Me and Within
(25 Minutes)

If you are in a larger group, break into groups of four to six for this discussion time. Introduce yourselves to each other if necessary. Briefly tell the group about your extended family. How far apart are you all geographically? How often do you see one another?

1. Read or review together the story about Daisy and her family in chapter 6 on pages 75–79 in the book. Daisy grows up with an abusive, alcoholic father, whom she refuses to forgive even as he lies on his deathbed, awaiting reconciliation. Daisy's daughter Margaret becomes a mother and breaks off her relationship with her son because she disapproves of his behavior. The son, Michael, experiences several broken relationships with women, the last ending in a bitter divorce.

   How does this story hit you? Is it surprising to hear of three generations of such blatant unforgiveness? How common do you think this kind of unforgiveness is among family members?

   Has your own family, in the past or present, exhibited similar instances of unforgiveness? Use discretion as you tell the others. You may want to refrain from using names.

   Is unforgiveness learned? What makes this cycle keep its power from one generation to the next? If Daisy had forgiven her father, do you think Margaret would be more likely to forgive her son today?

If a person is a committed Christian who genuinely loves God, why is forgiveness still so difficult at times? Think of instances in your life in which you were wronged. Why was, or is, forgiveness difficult?

• My pride—not only will I appear weak to the other and open to being wronged again but I will feel weak inside.
• My own pain and fear—to forgive would mean to let go of my pain and fear. I can't do that; I still feel them so strongly. Forgiveness would be merely an act.
• I feel a need to teach a lesson. If a person wrongs me and I forgive, I've offered an easy way out and increased the chances that the person will hurt someone else the same way he or she hurt me.
• I feel a need to stand against sin. In forgiving, it feels as if I am condoning the wrong behavior that is continuing in this person's life.
• Unforgiveness is the only way I can retain any power. If I forgive, I will be taken advantage of again, and I've lost any power to influence the other person.

On page 92 in the book, Henri Nouwen describes the inner tension that forgiveness involves. He describes God's heart, in forgiving, as "completely empty of self-seeking." This kind of forgiveness, he says, "calls me to keep stepping over all my arguments that say forgiveness is unwise, unhealthy, and impractical." Do you identify with Nouwen's "arguments" against forgiveness? How do they play out in your mind?

When set against Jesus' words in Matthew 6:15, "If you do not forgive men their sins, your Father will not forgive your sins," how do your arguments stand up?

Read the three paragraphs about the Joseph story on pages 84–85 in the book, beginning with the words "A story from Genesis . . ." Now read Genesis 42:1–8, 18–26; 43:26–31; 45:1–11. Can you envision Joseph's struggle to forgive—the anger and love that each seemed overpowering? What do you think was going on inside his head?

Have you experienced this kind of struggle to forgive, feeling consumed by anger yet moved to forgive and love anyway? What did you do in the end? Did you make the right decision? Can you tell the group about your experience?

2. Consider Matthew 5:23–24: "Therefore, if you are offering your gift at the altar and there remember that your brother has something against you, leave your gift there in front of the altar. First go and be reconciled to your brother; then come and offer your gift."

How seriously do most Christians take this verse today? What does it mean for us in contemporary terms? Should we skip church if we have an unresolved conflict with someone? Should we refrain from serving in the church or in the community? Should we delay putting money in the offering plate? How important is forgiveness to God?

Think for a moment about the other side of forgiveness— from the perspective of the one needing to be forgiven. Consider Tolstoy, whom I talk about on page 85 in the book. He thought he was starting his marriage right by showing his fiancée his diaries, which spelled out in detail all his sexual dalliances. He wanted to begin marriage forgiven, but his confessions caused his wife a lifetime of consuming jealousy. Are we ever wrong in confessing? Is it biblical to confess if what we confess makes things worse rather than better? How much honesty is too much?

3. Review the words of Dietrich Bonhoeffer, persecuted in Nazi Germany, and Sam Moffat, missionary in Communist China, on pages 89–90 in the book. "If I have no forgiveness for the Communists, then I have no message at all." Have you thought about the idea that forgiveness is the most significant way others see the gospel in you? How does that idea make you feel?

See Helmut Thielicke's words on page 91 in the book. "Both of us say to ourselves, 'The other fellow has to make the first move.' . . . I am always on the point of forgiving . . . but I never forgive. I am far too just." Breaking the cycle of ungrace means taking the initiative. Do you more often take the initiative or more often wait for the other to make the first move? With your spouse? Your friend? Your parent? Your child? Your sibling? You may want to take a few moments to think silently about this question, rather than discussing your answers.

4. Despite its rightness, forgiveness is not easy nor completely satisfying. Nagging injustices remain, and the wounds still cause pain. I have to approach God again and again, yielding to him the residue of what I thought I had committed to him long ago.

   Is there a person in your life whom you have forgiven but whose wrong toward you still causes pain and whom you sometimes wonder whether you've fully forgiven? Think about this for a moment, and discuss if you'd like. We will bring it to God in the prayer time that follows.

Do you have any prayer needs to express to the group?

God's Song of Grace to Me
(10–15 Minutes)

Listen together to music that draws us to forgiveness. Close your eyes and let God move in you and speak of the power of forgiveness in your life. Then sit in silence for several minutes, praying, meditating, or reflecting on today's study. You can write in your journal or in the space provided. You may want to add on to the prayer printed below.

Grace Notes

Listen together to the song "Beyond Justice to Mercy" by Susan Ashton. The song is on her CD or cassette titled *Wakened by the Wind* (Sparrow, 1991). The song is based on James 2:12–13. It speaks of disagreements, angry hearts, and bitter words. Ashton sings of choosing love and moving from justice to mercy.

If you'd prefer, listen to George Strait's song "Love without End, Amen," on his CD or cassette titled *Livin' It Up* (MCA, 1990). The song speaks movingly of a father's endless, unconditional love for his child.

If you do not have access to Susan Ashton or George Strait, sing with a piano, guitar, or *a capella* the praise song "Freely, Freely." The words read:

> God forgave my sin in Jesus' name,
> I've been born again in Jesus' name,
> and in Jesus' name I come to you,
> to share his love as he told me to.
> He said . . . 'Freely, freely you have received,
> freely, freely give.
> Go in my name and because you believe,
> others will know that I live.'

God, I keep coming back to this issue of forgiveness. At times

I try to ignore it and live on. I don't like thinking about the places in my life where forgiveness hasn't happened. Or where it needs to happen again. Sometimes I forgive easily. Other times even the thought of forgiving seems repugnant. My reluctance becomes a poison, eating away at my insides. In these times I'm not really blocking out the pain. It's you I'm blocking out. Help me understand. Help me want to forgive. And then, Lord, help me know how.

Joining in the Song of Grace

- This week pray about one area in your life where forgiveness needs to happen. This could concern a person, a group, yourself, or God. Know that the first step in forgiving is releasing your pain or anger to God, even if you may not feel ready to reconcile with others.
- Consider reading the book *My First White Friend* by Patricia Raybon (New York: Viking Penguin, 1996). She tells the story of how her racial hatred became hatred for herself. "The price of hating other human beings is loving oneself less," Raybon says. "I was believing you could carry animosity for another person in your heart and still feel okay about yourself. It doesn't work."[1] In her book Raybon writes extensively and profoundly about forgiveness.

- Other books about forgiveness you may want to consider reading are: *Not by the Sword* by Kathryn Watterson (New York: Simon & Schuster, 1995); *Forgive and Forget* by Lewis B. Smedes (San Francisco: Harper & Row, 1984); *The Art of Forgiving* by Lewis B. Smedes (New York: Random House, 1996).

Background Music of Grace This Week
(Optional)

Use the following Bible passages in your quiet moments this week as you reflect on God's grace through forgiveness.

Day 1: 2 Samuel 11:1–27
Day 2: 2 Samuel 12:1–25
Day 3: Psalm 51
Day 4: Psalm 32
Day 5: Colossians 3:1–17

Why Forgive?

Chapter 8

—✦—

The scandal of forgiveness confronts anyone who agrees to a moral cease-fire just because someone says, "I'm sorry." When I feel wronged, I can contrive a hundred reasons against forgiveness. *He needs to learn a lesson. I don't want to encourage irresponsible behavior. I'll let her stew for a while; it will do her good. She needs to learn that actions have consequences. I was the wronged party—it's not up to me to make the first move. How can I forgive if he's not even sorry?* I marshal my arguments until something happens to wear down my resistance. When I finally soften to the point of granting forgiveness, it seems a capitulation, a leap from hard logic to mushy sentiment.

Why do I ever make such a leap? I have already mentioned one factor that motivates me as a Christian: I am commanded to, as the child of a Father who forgives. But Christians have no monopoly on forgiveness. Why do any of us, Christian or unbeliever alike, choose this unnatural act? I can identify at least three pragmatic reasons, and the more I ponder these reasons for forgiveness, the more I recognize in them a logic that seems not only "hard" but foundational.

First, forgiveness alone can halt the cycle of blame and pain, breaking the chain of ungrace. In the New Testament the most common Greek word for forgiveness means, literally, to release, to hurl away, to free yourself.

The word *resentment* expresses what happens if the cycle goes uninterrupted. It means, literally, "to feel again": resentment clings to the past, relives it over and over, picks each fresh scab so that the wound never heals. This pattern doubtless began with the very first couple on earth. "Think of all the squabbles Adam and Eve must have had in the course of their nine hundred years," wrote Martin Luther. "Eve would say, 'You ate the apple,' and Adam would retort, 'You gave it to me.'"

Forgiveness offers a way out. It does not settle all questions of blame and fairness—often it pointedly evades those questions—but it does allow a relationship to start over, to begin anew. In that way, said Solzhenitsyn, we differ from all animals. Not our capacity to think, but our capacity to repent and to forgive makes us different. Only humans can perform that most unnatural act, which transcends the relentless law of nature.

If we do not transcend nature, we remain bound to the people we cannot forgive, held in their vise grip. This principle applies even when one party is wholly innocent and the other wholly to blame, for the innocent party will bear the wound until he or she can find a way to release it—and forgiveness is the only way.

We forgive not merely to fulfill some higher law of morality; we do it for ourselves. As Lewis Smedes points out, "The first and often the only person to be healed by forgiveness is the person who does the forgiveness. . . . When we genuinely forgive, we set a prisoner free and then discover that the prisoner we set free was us."

~

The second great power of forgiveness is that it can loosen the stranglehold of guilt in the perpetrator.

A member of the Ku Klux Klan, the Grand Dragon Larry Trapp of Lincoln, Nebraska, made national headlines in 1992 when he renounced his hatred, tore down his Nazi flags, and destroyed his many cartons of hate literature. As Kathryn Watterson recounts in the book *Not by the Sword,* Trapp had been won over by the forgiving love of a Jewish cantor and his family. Though Trapp had sent them vile pamphlets mocking big-nosed

Jews and denying the Holocaust, though he had threatened violence in phone calls made to their home, though he had targeted their synagogue for bombing, the cantor's family consistently responded with compassion and concern. Diabetic since childhood, Trapp was confined to a wheelchair and rapidly going blind; the cantor's family invited Trapp into their home to care for him. "They showed me such love that I couldn't help but love them back," Trapp later said. He spent his last months of life seeking forgiveness from Jewish groups, the NAACP, and the many individuals he had hated.

Magnanimous forgiveness allows the possibility of transformation in the guilty party. Lewis Smedes cautions that forgiveness is not the same as pardon: you may forgive one who wronged you and still insist on a just punishment for that wrong. If you can bring yourself to the point of forgiveness, though, you will release its healing power both in you and in the person who wronged you.

Forgiveness—undeserved, unearned—can cut the cords and let the oppressive burden of guilt roll away. The New Testament shows a resurrected Jesus leading Peter by the hand through a three-fold ritual of forgiveness. Peter need not go through life with the guilty, hangdog look of one who had betrayed the Son of God. Oh, no. On the backs of such transformed sinners Christ would build his church.

⁓

Forgiveness breaks the cycle of blame and loosens the stranglehold of guilt. It accomplishes these two things through a remarkable linkage, placing the forgiver on the same side as the party who did the wrong. Through it we realize we are not as different from the wrongdoer as we would like to think. "I also am other than what I imagine myself to be. To know this is forgiveness," said Simone Weil.

It occurred to me that the gracious miracle of God's forgiveness was made possible because of the linkage that occurred when God came to earth in Christ. Somehow God had to come to terms with these creatures he desperately wanted to love—but how? Experientially, God did not know what it was like to be tempted to sin, to have a trying day. On earth, living among us, he learned what it was like. He put himself on our side.

The Music of Grace in God's Word

Wait until you are instructed in the next section to read together the following passages from the Bible.

Mark 14:66–72
John 21:4–19

The Harmony of Grace Around Me and Within
(25 Minutes)

If you are in a larger group, break into groups of four to six for this discussion time. Introduce yourselves to each other if necessary. Tell the group about a pet you now own or have owned in the past. What is, or was, your biggest challenge in taking care of your pet?

1. Read the first six paragraphs of chapter 8 in the book, on Jeffrey Dahmer, the mass murderer who abused and then killed seventeen young men. While in prison Dahmer experienced a seemingly genuine conversion to Christ. He was later killed by a fellow prisoner. What is your reaction to the question of whether Dahmer could have been forgiven by God for his crimes?

2. Look now at some daily instances of forgiveness between people—spouses blaming one another for missing a mother's birthday; spouses sleeping in separate rooms for months after a wife forgets to replenish the bath soap; spouses sleeping apart for decades after fighting over how to care for a child; and a husband who sawed a house in half after fighting with his wife over the purchase of sugar. (These stories are found on pages 97–98 in the book. You may want to read them together to refresh your memory.)

These stories may sound ridiculous, yet the initial offenses are no different from the ones we encounter with our loved ones regularly. The choices we make daily about forgiveness determine the relationship for the days and months ahead. When you experience similar offenses with a spouse, family member, or friend, what is your typical reaction?

- I usually blow up, we fight about it, and then we forgive relatively quickly and it's over.
- I usually blow up, we fight about it, and then it takes a lot of work and a period of hard feelings before forgiveness happens.
- I don't react, in order to protect the relationship, but I carry a lot of hurt inside.
- I usually move on, faking kindness but hanging on to my anger.
- I pull away and use the silent treatment. Sometimes forgiveness happens; sometimes it doesn't.
- I usually forgive quickly. It's easier than the pain of not forgiving.
- Other: _____

3. We remain bound to the people we cannot forgive, held in their vise grip. This principle applies even when one party is wholly innocent and the other wholly to blame, for *the innocent party will bear the wound until he or she can find a way to release it*—and forgiveness is the only

way. One immigrant rabbi made an astonishing statement: "Before coming to America, I had to forgive Adolf Hitler," he said. "I did not want to bring Hitler inside me to my new country."

Have you been the innocent party and had to face forgiving the one to blame, when maybe that person wasn't even admitting wrong or requesting forgiveness? Maybe you are facing a situation like this now. How do you respond to the preceding paragraph? Discuss if you'd like, or consider quietly.

4. Review the stories of two Ku Klux Klan members on pages 100–1 in the book. Put yourself in the shoes of the Jewish family in the second story, who took Klan Grand Dragon Larry Trapp into their home and cared for him as he went blind. After the cruel anti-Semitic mail he had sent, his violent threats against the family, and his plans to bomb their synagogue, why would this family have treated Larry Trapp so lovingly? What would your reaction to Trapp have been?

Review the story of Jean Valjean in *Les Misérables* on pages 101–2 in the book. Read it together if you need to refresh your memory. Jean Valjean, after his prison release, was granted a night's stay in a bishop's home. After stealing silver from the bishop and being apprehended and forced to return to the bishop's home with the police, Valjean was given the silver candlesticks in addition to what he'd already stolen. The bishop denied before the police that Valjean had stolen anything, assuring instead that the silver was a gift. This act changed Jean Valjean's life forever.

How does this story impact you? If forgiveness isn't natural, how do people like the bishop and the Jewish family exhibit such extraordinary forgiveness? What would it take for a person to respond with this kind of ready and complete forgiveness? A onetime decision? A learned habit of forgiveness? Inner transformation by God?

Can you imagine yourself offering that kind of forgiveness? Have you ever received it? From another person? From God?

Review the story of Rebecca on pages 104–6 in the book. After enduring her pastor husband's involvement with prostitutes, and his eventual abandonment of her for another woman, Rebecca was faced with showing compassion toward her ex-husband's new wife. Can you relate to Rebecca's process of forgiveness: her realization that unless she forgave, her children would inherit her anger; her prayers filled with vengeance toward her ex-husband; her final release of her ex-husband to God for "what he deserved"; her verbal act of forgiveness to her ex-husband and his wife; and her own release of her bitter feelings? How can you relate?

5. Read together Mark 14:66–72 and John 21:4–19, the story of Peter's denial of Jesus, and Jesus' reinstatement of Peter. Can you think of a time when, like Peter in the Mark passage, you said or did something and later realized how hurtful you'd been toward another person? How did you feel? Like you'd strained the relationship? Like you'd cut yourself off from the relationship? Like you'd set yourself up for retaliation?

Now imagine that, similar to what Jesus did, that person had invited you to a meal, asked you to bring something, and during the meal expressed interest in the future of the relationship. How would you have felt?

6. Read the quote by Lewis Smedes on pages 102–3 in the book. Smedes says, "When you forgive someone, you slice away the wrong from the person who did it. You disengage that person from his hurtful act. You recreate him. . . . You think of him now not as the person who hurt you, but a person who needs you. . . . Once you branded him as a person powerful in evil, but now you see him as a person weak in his needs."

There are two sides to forgiveness. Do Smedes' words reflect how you would have felt in the previous question, sharing a meal with the one you'd hurt? Now imagine you are the one doing the forgiving. How do Smedes' words, on changing your perspective of the person who has wronged you, help in the act of forgiveness? In doing this, are you just playing mind games, or are you allowing yourself to see things as they really are?

Do Smedes' words help you understand how God views you as he forgives you?

Do you have any prayer requests to express to the group?

God's Song of Grace to Me
(10–15 Minutes)

Listen together to music that encourages us to forgive. Close your eyes and pray for God's transforming power of forgiveness to fill you. Then sit silently for a few more minutes, meditating on God's words to you, journaling, or writing a prayer.

Grace Notes

Listen together to the song "Forgive One Another" on the CD or cassette titled *Songs from the Red Letters* by Faithful Heart (Maranatha, 1996). Kelly Willard and Lenny LeBlanc sing of following, as God's children, in the pattern of forgiveness he has set for us.

If you do not have access to Faithful Heart or prefer an alternate piece of music, obtain a CD or cassette of the "Hymn of Praise" in Felix Mendelssohn's *Symphony No. 2.* This hymn does not speak specifically of forgiveness; however, Mendelssohn's life was a testimony to forgiveness. His family was of Jewish descent, but due to deep prejudice toward Jews in Europe, Mendelssohn's father raised his children in the Christian faith. As a young boy, Mendelssohn was teased for being a Jew worshiping Christ, yet he never resented his new faith. Rather he embraced it wholeheartedly and held a lifelong respect for the Bible.[1] He was ever grateful to God, as his hymn expresses.

If you cannot locate a taped version of the "Hymn of Praise" by Mendelssohn, find the hymn "Now Thank We All Our God" (which has the same words as Mendelssohn's hymn) in a hymnal and sing together with piano, guitar, or *a capella.*

Joining in the Song of Grace

- Continue to pray this week about an area in your life where forgiveness needs to happen. If family or friends are involved, consider the traditional method of forgiveness used in Hawaii. The process is called *ho'oponopono,* meaning "setting to right." Native Hawaiians have long encouraged this ritual to maintain harmony and solve conflict within a family. The process can work for community relationships as well.

Ho'oponopono starts with a prayer, or *pule,* asking God for help in solving the family trouble. Then family members sit together in a circle or around a table and discuss the problem. They share how they have felt and why they have acted as they have. They trace the problem from beginning to end. They confess wrongs and offer restitution. Then they forgive one another, releasing each other and themselves. Finally, there is a *pani*—the problem is declared closed. In a closing prayer, they seek to reestablish harmony with God and ask God's forgiveness.[2]

If your family or friends are not able or willing to join you in this process, enter into it on your own. Pray; think about the issue and put some of your hurts on paper, maybe in a letter; confess your own wrongs; then forgive the one who offended you. Release your anger. Then commit your forgiveness to God and ask his forgiveness of you.

• Consider and pray about reconciliation as it relates to criminal justice. The Victim Offender Reconciliation Program (VORP), part of the Restorative Justice Ministries of the Center for Peacemaking and Conflict Studies at Fresno Pacific University, seeks a constructive community response for offenders who are willing to accept responsibility for their actions. The VORP Peacemaking Model calls for discussion and constructive activity until there is a mutual recognition among victim, community, and offender that an injustice has occurred. Equity is then restored (an activity that builds self-worth in the offender). An agreement is made regarding a constructive future (criminal activity stops only when an offender makes a deliberate decision). VORP calls for follow-up accountability and support. To learn more about the church-based VORP program, call 1-800-909-VORP.

Background Music of Grace This Week
(Optional)

Read the following Bible passages this week in your quiet moments as you reflect on forgiveness. Use these readings as your time allows.

Day 1: 1 Corinthians 13
Day 2: Hebrews 4:14–5:10
Day 3: 2 Corinthians 5:11–6:2
Day 4: Mark 14:66–72; John 21:4–19
Day 5: Luke 23:26–49; 1 Corinthians 13

Getting Even

Chapter 9

In the midst of the recent war in the former Yugoslavia, I picked up a book: *The Sunflower* by Simon Wiesenthal. The book centers on forgiveness, and I turned to it for insight into what role forgiveness might play globally—in, say, the moral quagmire that once was Yugoslavia.

In 1944 Wiesenthal was a young Polish prisoner of the Nazis. All together, eighty-nine of his Jewish relatives would die at the hands of the Nazis. Wiesenthal's prison detail was cleaning rubbish out of a hospital for German casualties, when one day he was brought to the room of a dying SS officer. "My name is Karl," said a raspy voice. "I must tell you of this horrible deed—tell you because you are a Jew."

Karl begged Wiesenthal to listen to what he had just experienced in the Ukraine. In one town, Karl's unit stumbled onto booby traps that killed thirty of their soldiers. As an act of revenge the SS rounded up three hundred Jews, herded them into a three-story house, doused it with gasoline, and fired grenades at it. Karl and his men encircled the house, their guns drawn to shoot anyone who tried to escape.

"The screams from the house were horrible," he said, reliving the moment. "I saw a man with a small child in his arms. His clothes were alight. By his side stood a woman, doubtless the mother of the child. With his free hand the man covered the child's eyes, then he jumped into the street. Seconds later the mother followed. Then from the other windows fell burning bodies. We shot . . . Oh God!

"I know that what I have told you is terrible. In the long nights while I have been waiting for death, time and time again I have longed to talk about it to a Jew and beg forgiveness from him. Only I didn't know whether there were any Jews left . . . I know what I am asking is almost too much for you, but without your answer I cannot die in peace."[1]

Simon Wiesenthal, an architect in his early twenties, now a prisoner dressed in a shabby uniform marked with the yellow Star of David, felt the immense crushing burden of his race bear down on him.

"At last I made up my mind," Wiesenthal writes, "and without a word I left the room."

~

Simon Wiesenthal lived on to be liberated from a death camp by American troops. The scene in the hospital room haunted him like a ghost. Finally, more than twenty years after the war had ended, he wrote down the story and sent it to the brightest ethical minds he knew: Jew and Gentile, Catholic, Protestant, and irreligious. "What would you have done in my place?" he asked them.

Of the thirty-two men and women who responded, only six said that Wiesenthal had erred in not forgiving the German. According to the others, Wiesenthal had done the right thing, for what moral or legal authority had he to forgive crimes done to someone else?

As I read the eloquent replies to Wiesenthal's question I was struck by the terrible, crystalline logic of unforgiveness. In a world of unspeakable atrocity, forgiveness indeed seems unjust, unfair, irrational. Individuals and families must learn to forgive, yes, but how do such high-minded principles apply in a case like Nazi Germany?

Is it too much to expect that the high ethical ideals of the gospel—of which forgiveness lies at the core—might transpose into the brutal world of politics and international diplomacy?

The strongest argument in favor of grace is the alternative, a world of ungrace. The strongest argument for forgiveness is the alternative, a permanent state of unforgiveness. Where unforgiveness reigns, as essayist Lance Morrow has pointed out, a Newtonian law comes into play: For every atrocity there must be an equal and opposite atrocity.

As I write this, nearly two million Hutu refugees sit idly in refugee camps on the borders of Rwanda, refusing all entreaties to go home. Shouting through bullhorns, their leaders warn them not to trust Tutsi promises that "all is forgiven." They will murder you, say the Hutu leaders. They will seek revenge for the five hundred thousand murders we committed on the Tutsis.

In the logic of unforgiveness, not to strike against the enemy would betray ancestors and the sacrifices they made. There is one major flaw in the law of revenge, however: it never settles the score.

Forgiveness may be unfair—it is, by definition—but at least it provides a way to halt the juggernaut of retribution. Today, as I write, violence is either breaking out or smoldering just under the surface between China and Taiwan, India and Pakistan, Russia and Chechnya, Great Britain and Ireland, and especially between Jews and Arabs in the Middle East. Each of these disputes traces back decades, centuries, or, in the case of the Jews and Arabs, millennia. Each side strives to overcome an injustice from the past, to right a perceived wrong.

We have many vivid demonstrations of the law of unforgiveness. In Shakespeare's and Sophocles' historical tragedies, bodies litter the stage. Francis Ford Coppola's *Godfather* trilogy and Clint Eastwood's *Unforgiven* illustrate the same law.

Yet history shows that forgiveness can indeed be a powerful weapon in the making of peace. Great leaders—Lincoln, Gandhi, King, Rabin, and Sadat come to mind, all of whom paid the ultimate price for defying the law of ungrace—can help create a national climate that leads to reconciliation. How different would modern history be if Sadat and not Saddam ruled Iraq. Or if a Lincoln emerged from the ruins of Yugoslavia.

Politics deals with externals: borders, wealth, crimes. Authentic forgiveness deals with the evil in a person's heart, something for which politics has no cure. Virulent evil (racism, ethnic hatred) spreads through society like an airborne disease; one cough infects a whole busload. The cure, like a vaccine, must be applied one person at a time. When moments of grace do occur, the world must pause, fall silent, and acknowledge that indeed forgiveness offers a kind of cure. Grace has its own power.

The Music of Grace in God's Word

Wait until you are instructed to read together the following passages from the Bible.

Psalm 51
Psalm 130

The Harmony of Grace Around Me and Within
(25 Minutes)

If you are in a larger group, break into groups of four to six for this discussion time. Introduce yourselves to each other if necessary. Tell the group briefly about a time you were very sick. What was wrong? How vulnerable did you feel during this time?

1. Talk about the story of Simon Wiesenthal, printed at the beginning of this session (you can find a more detailed version in the book on pages 109–11). If Wiesenthal had asked for your response to his question, what would you have said? (Try to answer as you would have before you began this study—don't feel a need to give the "right" answer. We can examine the issue more deeply if we try to reveal what has really been inside us.)

   Have you ever, like Wiesenthal, refused one who asked your forgiveness? Has anyone ever refused your request for forgiveness?

   One philosopher who replied to Wiesenthal's question said, "One cannot, and should not go around happily killing and torturing and then, when the moment has come, simply ask, and receive, forgiveness." Karl felt remorse. What about the person you might have refused to forgive? Did that person feel remorse? Can one ask and receive forgiveness without really feeling remorse?

   Read Psalm 51 and Psalm 130 together as a group. As you read, imagine that these are the words of Karl, the SS officer, as he lay in his hospital room, waiting to die—or of the person you wouldn't forgive. Do these words cause you to view Karl, and the person you wouldn't forgive, differently? What parts of these psalms particularly speak to this issue?

Have you ever prayed a prayer similar to these psalms?

2. Consider the tension between justice and forgiveness. Is
   the way of forgiveness an appropriate choice for leaders at
   the national and international level? Jimmy Carter, founder
   of the Carter Center, has done some of the most significant work of our time in international peacemaking. Yet
   Carter says, "A president isn't in a position to sacrifice his
   country's interests and commit the act of selfless love. . . .
   The highest calling of a society is justice. It wouldn't have
   been possible as President to exercise unselfish love. I
   couldn't make that sacrifice as the leader of a nation. But as
   an individual, in my role now, I can do it."[2] Carter's words
   reflect the great responsibility national leaders carry. Is forgiveness only appropriate in some situations?

   Consider the modern-day national and international conflicts mentioned in the second half of the summary in this
   session, or on pages 114–16 in the book. In the logic of
   unforgiveness, not to strike against the enemy would
   betray ancestors and the sacrifices they made. Where is
   the hope for an end to the conflicts?

3. Read the story about Helmut Thielicke on page 117 in the book. He tells of his first Bible study meeting as a new pastor in a German state church. Three elderly women joined him, while outside in the streets marched Hitler's Youth Corps. "The kingdom of heaven is like a grain of mustard seed . . . ," Thielicke had to remind himself. When have you felt like this pastor—weak and outnumbered by forces that would seemingly overpower you? Maybe as a parent trying to raise moral children? As a student in a secular environment? As an employee in a competitive or unethical workplace? As a sexually pure person in a culture full of temptation?

4. Review together the story of Gordon Wilson on pages 117–18 in the book. Wilson and his daughter, Marie, were the victims of an IRA bombing near Belfast. As they lay beneath five feet of concrete and brick, Marie's last words were, "Daddy, I love you very much." Later, speaking from his hospital bed, Wilson said, "I have lost my daughter, but I bear no grudge. Bitter talk is not going to bring Marie Wilson back to life. I shall pray, tonight and every night, that God will forgive them."

Meeting with the IRA, Wilson forgave them and said, "I know that you've lost loved ones, just like me. Surely, enough is enough. Enough blood has been spilled." How does Wilson's story speak to you? Have you known anyone personally who forgave some such "unforgivable" act?

5. Look again at Psalm 51. Read verses 1–2 and 10–12. What are the implications concerning forgiveness if we pray this psalm in sincerity?

Do you have any prayer needs you would like to share with the group?

God's Song of Grace to Me
(10–15 Minutes)

Listen to some music about grace together, and then spend some time in the quiet with God. You may want to meditate on the words of Psalm 51:10–12:

Create in me a pure heart, O God, and renew a steadfast spirit within me. Do not cast me from your presence or take your Holy Spirit from me. Restore to me the joy of your salvation and grant me a willing spirit, to sustain me.

Or you may want to pray the prayer of Psalm 130. If you use this time to write, use your journal or the space provided.

Grace Notes

Listen together to the song "Love Brought Me Back" by Helen Baylor. It is found on her CD or cassette titled *Love Brought Me Back* (Word, 1996). You may feel the urge to get up and dance. Feel free to do so—it might be an appropriate release after weighty discussion!

If you do not have access to Helen Baylor, sing together the praise song "Shine, Jesus, Shine" or find in a hymnal the song

"Cleanse Me," which begins with the words "Search me, O God." Sing with a piano, guitar, or *a capella.*

Joining in the Song of Grace

- As you read the newspaper, watch the news, and talk with others this week, pay special attention to the conflicts that are discussed, whether they are between nations, groups, families, or individuals. What is at the root of the conflict? Is there a history of conflict between the parties? What could have stopped the current conflict?
- Continue to pray about personal issues of forgiveness. Continue working on the steps to forgiveness outlined in the last session's "Joining in the Song of Grace" section. Arrange a meeting for reconciliation if necessary, or write a letter for mailing or for private expression. Risk the sharp edges of reconciliation by moving into the soft heart of forgiveness.

Background Music of Grace This Week
(Optional)

Read the following Bible passages this week in your quiet moments. Reflect on these readings as your time allows.

Day 1: Matthew 7:1–5
Day 2: Matthew 13:31–35
Day 3: Matthew 13:44–46
Day 4: Psalm 51
Day 5: Psalm 130

The Arsenal of Grace

Chapter 10

‿

Walter Wink tells of two peacemakers who visited a group of Polish Christians ten years after the end of World War II. "Would you be willing to meet with other Christians from West Germany?" the peacemakers asked. "They want to ask forgiveness for what Germany did to Poland during the war and to begin to build a new relationship."

At first there was silence. Then one Pole spoke up. "What you are asking is impossible. Each stone of Warsaw is soaked in Polish blood! We cannot forgive!"

Before the group parted, however, they said the Lord's Prayer together. When they reached the words "forgive us our sins as we forgive . . . ," everyone stopped praying. Tension swelled in the room. The Pole who had spoken so vehemently said, "I must say yes to you. I could no more pray the Our Father, I could no longer call myself a Christian, if I refuse to forgive. Humanly speaking, I cannot do it, but God will give us his strength!" Eighteen months later the Polish and West German Christians met together in Vienna, establishing friendships that continue to this day.

‿

Paul Tillich once defined forgiveness as remembering the past in order that it might be forgotten—a principle that applies to nations as well as individuals. Though forgiveness is never easy, and may take generations, what else can break the chains that enslave people to their historical past?

I will never forget a scene that I witnessed in the Soviet Union in October 1991. At the time, the Soviet empire was unraveling, Mikhail Gorbachev was hanging on to office by a string, and Boris Yeltsin was consolidating power by the day. I accompanied a delegation of Christians who met with Russia's leaders in response to their plea for help in "restoring morality" to their country.

Although Gorbachev and all the government officials we visited had received us warmly, old-timers in our group warned us to expect different treatment the evening we visited KGB headquarters.

"Meeting with you here tonight," General Nikolai Stolyarov, Vice-Chairman of the KGB, began, "is a plot twist that could not have been conceived by the wildest fiction writer." Then he startled us by saying, "We here in the USSR realize that too often we've been negligent in accepting those of the Christian faith. But political questions cannot be decided until there is sincere repentance, a return to faith by the people. That is the cross I must bear. In the study of scientific atheism, there was the idea that religion divides people. Now we see the opposite: love for God can only unite."

Our heads spun. Where did he learn the phrase "bear a cross"? And the other word—*repentance?*

Stolyarov explained in measured tones: "I have spoken of repentance. This is an essential step. There can be no *perestroika* apart from repentance. The time has come to repent of that past. We have broken the Ten Commandments, and for this we pay today."

Abruptly, the meeting took a more personal turn as Alex Leonovich, the translator, rose to speak. A native of Byelorussia, he had escaped during Stalin's reign of terror and had emigrated to the United States. For forty-six years he had been broadcasting Christian programs, often jammed, back to the land of his birth. He knew personally many Christians who had been tortured and persecuted for their faith. For him, to be translating such a message of reconciliation from a high official of the KGB was bewildering and nearly incomprehensible.

Alex spoke slowly and softly to General Stolyarov. "General, many members of my family suffered because of this organization," Alex said. "I myself had to leave the land that I loved. My uncle, who was very dear to me, went to a labor camp in Siberia and never returned. General, you say that you repent. Christ taught us how to respond. On behalf of my family, on behalf of my uncle who died in the Gulag, I forgive you."

And then Alex Leonovich, Christian evangelist, reached over to General Nikolai Stolyarov, the Vice-Chairman of the KGB, and gave him a Russian bear hug. While they embraced, Stolyarov whispered something to Alex, and not until later did we learn what he said. "Only two times in my life have I cried. Once was when my mother died. The other is tonight."

For the next decades—and perhaps centuries—the former Soviet Union will be confronting issues of forgiveness. With good reason, Russians do not trust each other or their government. The past must be remembered before it can be overcome.

Even so, overcoming history is possible, however slowly and imperfectly. The chains of ungrace can indeed snap. We in the United States have had experience with reconciliation on a national scale: archenemies in World War II, Germany and Japan are now two of our staunchest allies. Even more significantly, we fought a bloody Civil War that set family against family and the nation against itself.

After the Civil War, rather than punishing the South, Abraham Lincoln said, "Do I not destroy my enemies when I make them my friends?" setting forth instead a magnanimous plan of Reconstruction. Even more impressive are the steps toward reconciliation between white and black races, one of which used to *own* the other. The lingering effects of racism prove that it takes many years and much hard work to undo injustice. Still, every step African-Americans take toward participation as citizens implies a move toward forgiveness.

I grew up a racist. Although I am not yet fifty years old, I remember well when the South practiced a perfectly legal form of apartheid. Stores in downtown Atlanta had three rest rooms: White Men, White Women, and Colored. Motels and restaurants served white patrons only, and when the Civil Rights Act made such discrimination illegal, many owners shuttered their establishments.

When Congress passed the Civil Rights Act, our church founded a private school as a haven for whites, expressly barring all black students. We used to call Martin Luther King Jr. "Martin Lucifer Coon." We said that King was a card-carrying Communist, a Marxist agent who merely posed as a minister. Not until much later was I able to appreciate the moral strength of the man who, perhaps more than any other person, kept the South from outright racial war.

King deliberately stage-managed scenes of confrontation, accepting beatings, jailings, and other brutalities, because he believed a complacent nation would rally around his cause only when they saw the evil of racism manifest in its ugliest extreme. By forcing evil out into the open, King was attempting to tap into a national reservoir of moral outrage, a concept my friends and I were not equipped to understand.

King had developed a sophisticated strategy of war fought with grace, not gunpowder. He never refused to meet with his adversaries. He opposed policies but not personalities. Most importantly, he countered violence with nonviolence, and hatred with love. "Let us not seek to satisfy our thirst for freedom by drinking from the cup of bitterness and hatred," he exhorted his followers.

Their real goal, King said, was not to defeat the white man but "to awaken a sense of shame within the oppressor and challenge his false sense of superiority. . . . The end is reconciliation; the end is redemption; the end is the creation of the beloved community." And that is what Martin Luther King Jr. finally set into motion, even in die-hard racists like me. The power of grace disarmed my own stubborn evil.

～

Elton Trueblood notes that the image Jesus used to describe the church's destiny—"the gates of hell will not prevail against it"—is a metaphor of offense, not defense. Christians are storming the gates, and they will prevail. No matter how it looks at any given point in history, the gates guarding the powers of evil will not withstand an assault by grace.

The Cold War, says former Senator Sam Nunn, ended "not in a nuclear inferno, but in a blaze of candles in the churches of Eastern Europe." Several hundred thousand people took part in candlelight processions in East Germany, singing hymns and praying. Police and soldiers with all their weapons seemed powerless against such a force. Ultimately, on the night a similar march in East Berlin attracted one million protesters, the hated Berlin Wall came tumbling down without a shot being fired. A huge banner appeared across a Leipzig street: *Wir danken Dir, Kirche* (We thank you, church).

Like a gale of pure air driving out stagnant clouds of pollution, peaceful revolution spread across the globe. In 1989 alone ten nations comprising half a billion people experienced nonviolent revolutions. In many of these, the Christian minority played a crucial role.

Then in 1994 came the most surprising revolution of all, surprising because nearly everyone expected bloodshed. In South Africa, after a mediation team led by Henry Kissinger had abandoned all hope of convincing the Inkatha Freedom Party to participate in elections, a Christian diplomat from Kenya met privately with all the principals, prayed with them, and helped change their minds.

Nelson Mandela broke the chain of ungrace when he emerged from twenty-six years of imprisonment with a message of forgiveness and reconciliation, not revenge. F. W. De Klerk himself felt what he later described as "a strong sense of calling." He told his congregation that God was calling him to save all the people of South Africa, even though he knew that would mean rejection by his own people.

Black leaders insisted that De Klerk apologize for racial apartheid. He balked, because the people who had started the policy included his own father. But Bishop Desmond Tutu believed it essential that the process of reconciliation in South Africa begin with forgiveness, and he would not relent. According to Tutu, "One lesson we should be able to teach the world, and that we should be able to teach the people of Bosnia, Rwanda, and Burundi, is that we are ready to forgive." Eventually, De Klerk did apologize.

Because it goes against human nature, forgiveness must be taught and practiced, as one would practice any difficult craft. "Forgiveness is not just an occasional act: it is a permanent attitude," said Martin Luther King Jr. What greater gift could Christians give to the world than the forming of a culture that upholds grace and forgiveness?

The Music of Grace in God's Word

Read together the following passage from the Bible.

Matthew 16.13–20

The Harmony of Grace Around Me and Within
(25 Minutes)

If you are in a larger group, break into groups of four to six for this discussion time. Introduce yourselves to one another if necessary. Tell the group about a time you locked yourself out of your car or house. Where were your keys? Who rescued you?

1. Look at the story of the Polish Christians who prayed the Lord's Prayer, printed at the beginning of this session. "I could no longer call myself a Christian, if I refuse to

forgive," the Pole said. "Humanly speaking, I cannot do it, but God will give us his strength!" At the moment the Pole spoke, did he *want* to forgive? Were his words spoken more from his mind or his heart?

When we act in integrity to the gospel, should we wait for healing to occur first within ourselves before acting, or should we act and expect the healing to follow?

2. Look at the statement drafted by the East German parliament after the first free elections:

> We, the first freely elected parliamentarians of the GDR ... on behalf of the citizens of this land, admit responsibility for the humiliation, expulsion and murder of Jewish men, women and children. We feel sorrow and shame, and acknowledge this burden of German history.... Immeasurable suffering was inflicted on the peoples of the world during the era of national socialism....We ask all the Jews of the world to forgive us. We ask the people of Israel to forgive us for the hypocrisy and hostility of official East German policies toward Israel and for the persecution and humiliation of Jewish citizens in our country after 1945 as well.

What do you think about this parliament accepting responsibility for actions that most of its members did not personally commit? Were they inappropriately seeking forgiveness that wasn't theirs to seek? Would a statement similar to the one above, offered by the U.S. government asking forgiveness of African-Americans for the years of slavery, be a positive step toward reconciliation between races?

If forgiveness involves remembering the past in order that it might be forgotten, of what value are Holocaust museums, the Vietnam memorial, documentaries on the Civil War, and the remains of a crumbled Berlin Wall? Have any of these or similar remembrances helped to bring the past to life for you and in turn bring about personal repentance or forgiveness?

I talk about my own experience with racism. Have you had a similar experience—perhaps you served in Vietnam or worked for a bad employer or had a difficult church experience—that forced you to struggle with issues of forgiveness and reconciliation?

3. Review the story of the KGB in the Soviet Union, printed at the beginning of this session. The story is found in more detail on pages 126–29 in the book. How could men who had been so evil for so long truly change? How could men who had been unchristian for so long suddenly understand

the core of the gospel? Would you have responded skeptically, like the Russian photographer? See Matthew 16:18.

Does this true story give you hope for a situation or relationship in your life that seems irreconcilable? If you'd like, tell the group about the situation.

4. Growing up, what were your parents' views on racism? What were your views? Have your views changed over time? Do you currently have close friends from other races?

"The end is reconciliation; the end is redemption; the end is the creation of the beloved community," said Martin Luther King Jr. You may live in a community without much racial diversity, and you may have never held racist attitudes. Even if that is the case, do you think it's important for you to do what you can to better understand the pain of those who have suffered racially? How could you do this?

5. Review the examples of how peaceful revolution helped change South Africa, printed at the beginning of this session. These are found in more detail on pages 135–37 in the book. As with the Soviet Union, it once seemed hopeless to expect change in South Africa. But healing change came, largely due to peaceful revolution, forgiveness, and the continuing work of reconciliation.

What cause or issue of injustice weighs most heavily in your life? Maybe racism? Abortion? Gender discrimination? Religious discrimination? Issues of poverty and wealth? Something else? What would a peaceful revolution on your part look like? Are you now engaging in a peaceful battle, with the goal of forgiveness and reconciliation? If not, how could you begin?

Do you have any prayer requests to share with the group?

God's Song of Grace to Me
(10–15 Minutes)

[Leader: During this part of the session, we will first listen to music. Afterward, instead of spending time together in silence, we will take part in a Benedictine-style service of forgiveness and reconciliation. Prepare for this ahead of time by gathering a punch bowl or serving bowl for each small group of four to six people. Groups of five or six may need two bowls, depending on the size of the bowls. Fill the bowls with water. If there are issues of reconciliation that need to be resolved in your church, study group, or community, consider inviting the appropriate parties to this session to take part in this service.]

Listen to a musical version of the Lord's Prayer together (see "Grace Notes," following). Close your eyes and ask God to prepare your heart as you listen. Then, staying in small groups of four to six, join in a Benedictine-style service of forgiveness and reconciliation. The leader or a designated person in each group will read Matthew 6:14–15, Luke 6:37–38, and Ephesians 4:31–5:2. Then take turns in the small group, identifying issues in which you need to forgive. If some people have private issues, spend a few moments in silence so they can speak of these to God. Then all of you will submerge your hands in the bowl of water. Each person's hands should be clasped together, as if holding the grievance. The leader or a designated person will pray for God's grace to forgive. Then pray together the Lord's Prayer. As you pray, open your hands in a symbolic gesture of releasing the grievance, choosing to forgive. This service can be a powerful and transforming physical act of forgiveness.

Grace Notes

Listen together to Tchaikovsky's *Pater Noster ("The Lord's Prayer")*. Many libraries will have a CD containing this piece and available for public use. If you do not have access to Tchaikovsky's version, find another recording of the Lord's Prayer, or find a version your group can sing together with the piano, guitar, or *a capella*.

Joining in the Song of Grace

- This week continue to pray about personal issues of forgiveness. If it would be helpful, make a practice each day this week of filling up your bathroom sink with water and praying with your cupped hands submerged in the water. Renew your commitment to forgiveness each day as you pray, releasing your hands and a grievance that again may have threatened to take hold in you.

- This week as you read the newspaper or listen to the radio or watch television, pay attention to news of countries that have experienced peaceful revolution—for instance, countries in the former Soviet Union, and countries in Eastern Europe. Pray for God's help as individuals and these governments continue in the process of reconciliation. Pay attention also to news of countries who are still plagued with conflict. Pray for a peaceful release of hostilities.
- Consider reading the book *Breaking Down Walls: A Model for Reconciliation in an Age of Racial Strife* by Raleigh Washington and Glen Kehrein. The book is available through Promise Keepers by calling 1-800-456-7594. Or read *More Than Equals* by John Perkins and Chris Rice (Downers Grove, Ill.: InterVarsity Press, 1993).

Background Music of Grace This Week
(Optional)

Use the following Bible passages in your quiet moments this week as you reflect on God's grace. Use these readings as your time allows.

Day 1: 2 Corinthians 4:7–18
Day 2: Ephesians 1:15–23
Day 3: Ephesians 3:14–21
Day 4: 1 Peter 1:1–25
Day 5: 2 Peter 1:1–11

Week Eight

Oddballs, Jesus, and Me

Chapters 11–13

In the 1960s a Yale Divinity School graduate and Southerner named Will Campbell befriended a Harvard Divinity School student named Jonathan Daniels. Campbell and Daniels were each involved in the civil rights crusade. Campbell's theology was undergoing some testing in those days. Much of the opposition to his work came from "good Christians." Campbell found allies more easily among agnostics, socialists, and a few devout Northerners.

"In ten words or less, what's the Christian message?" one agnostic had challenged him. The interlocutor was P. D. East, a renegade newspaper editor who viewed Christians as the enemy.

I said, "We're all bastards but God loves us anyway." . . .
He often reminded me of what I had said that day.

The definition stung P. D. East who, unbeknown to Campbell, was indeed illegitimate and had been called "bastard" all his life. (Campbell had meant "bastard" in a theological sense: we are illegitimate children "adopted" by God.) He put that definition to a ruthless test on the darkest day of Campbell's life, a day when an Alabama deputy sheriff named Thomas Coleman gunned down Campbell's twenty-six-year-old friend Jonathan Daniels.

That night, Campbell spoke with P. D. East and got "the most enlightening theological lesson I ever had in my life." P. D. pressed Campbell on whether his definition of faith could stand the test.

"Was Jonathan a bastard?" P. D. asked first. Campbell replied that though he was one of the most gentle guys he'd ever known, it's true that everyone is a sinner. In those terms, yes, he was a "bastard."

"All right. Is Thomas Coleman a bastard?" That question, Campbell found much easier to answer. You bet the murderer was a bastard.

Then P. D. pulled his chair close, placed his bony hand on Campbell's knee, and looked directly into his eyes. "Which one of these two bastards do you think God loves the most?" The question hit home, like an arrow to the heart.

> Suddenly everything became clear. Everything. It was a revelation. . . . I began to whimper. But the crying was interspersed with laughter. . . . I was laughing at myself, at twenty years of a ministry which had become, without my realizing it, a ministry of liberal sophistication. . . .
>
> I agreed that the notion that a man could go to a store, . . . fire a shotgun blast at one of them, tearing his lungs and heart and bowels from his body, . . . and that God would set him free is almost more than I could stand. But unless that is precisely the case then there is no Gospel, there is no Good News. Unless that is the truth we have only bad news, we are back with law alone.

What Will Campbell learned that night was a new insight into grace. The free offer of grace extends not just to the undeserving but to those who in fact deserve the *opposite*.

This message lodged so deep inside Will Campbell that he resigned his position with the National Council of Churches and became what he wryly calls "an apostle to the rednecks." He bought a farm in Tennessee, and today is as likely to spend his time among Klansmen and racists as among racial minorities and white liberals. A lot of people, he decided, were volunteering to help minorities; he knew of no one ministering to the Thomas Colemans of the world.

~

I once explored the following question with a congregation on a Sunday morning: "What did God have against lobster?" We looked at the laws detailed in Leviticus concerning clean and unclean foods. Then we looked at the story of Peter in Acts 10, where God gave a vision of a sheet filled with unclean animals and removed all prohibitions. Peter was shaken to the core. Yet why had God declared lobster and rabbits and camels, for instance, unclean in the first place?

After studying the various theories on Old Testament ritual laws, I have come up with an all-encompassing principle that, I believe, expresses the essence of the laws on uncleanness: No Oddballs Allowed. The Israelites' diet scrupulously excluded any abnormal or "oddball" animals, and the same principle applied also to "clean" animals used in worship. God wanted the unblemished of the flock. God demanded perfection; God deserved the best. No Oddballs Allowed.

The Old Testament applies a similar, far more troubling, ranking to people. It is one thing to label animals unclean and quite another to label people unclean, but Old Testament laws did not shrink from that step. In sum, those with damaged bodies or damaged family lines (bastards) failed to qualify: No Oddballs Allowed. Menstruating women, men who had recently had a nocturnal emission, women who had undergone childbirth, people with skin diseases or running sores, anyone who had touched a corpse—all these were declared ceremonially unclean.

When rumors spread that Jesus could be the long-awaited Messiah, pious Jews were more scandalized than galvanized. Had he not touched unclean persons, such as those suffering from leprosy? Had he not let a woman of ill repute wash his feet with her hair? He dined with tax collectors—one even joined his inner circle of the Twelve—and was notoriously lax about the rules of ritual cleanness and Sabbath observance.

Moreover, Jesus deliberately crossed into Gentile territory. He praised a Roman centurion as having more faith than anyone in

Israel. He healed a half-breed Samaritan with leprosy and had a lengthy conversation with a Samaritan woman. This woman became the first "missionary" appointed by Jesus and the first person to whom he openly revealed his identity as Messiah. Then Jesus culminated his time on earth by giving his disciples the "Great Commission," a command to take the gospel to unclean Gentiles.

Jesus' approach to "unclean" people dismayed his countrymen and, in the end, helped to get him crucified. In essence, Jesus canceled the cherished principle of the Old Testament, No Oddballs Allowed, replacing it with a new rule of grace: "We're all oddballs, but God loves us anyhow."

We ourselves can be agents of God's holiness, for God now dwells within us. In the midst of an unclean world we can stride, as Jesus did, seeking ways to be a source of holiness. The sick and the maimed are for us not hot spots of contamination but potential reservoirs of God's mercy. We are called upon to extend that mercy, to be conveyers of grace, not avoiders of contagion.

The shift that Jesus introduced has important consequences for every Christian. Jesus' revolution of grace affects me deeply in at least two ways.

First, it affects my access to God. Whereas Old Testament worshipers purified themselves before entering the temple and presented their offerings to God through a priest, in the Book of Acts God's followers were meeting in private homes and addressing God with the informal *Abba*. It was a familiar term of family affection, like "Daddy," and before Jesus no one would have thought of applying such a word to Yahweh, the Sovereign Lord of the Universe. After him, it became the standard word used by early Christians to address God in prayer.

The second way in which Jesus' revolution affects me centers on how we are to view "different" people. Jesus' example convicts me today, because I sense a subtle shift in the reverse direction. As society unravels and immorality increases, I hear calls from some Christians that we show less mercy and more morality, calls that hark back to the style of the Old Testament. Some Christians

I know have taken on the task of "moral exterminator" for the evil-infested society around them.

I share a deep concern for our society. I am struck, though, by the alternative power of mercy as demonstrated by Jesus, who came for the sick and not the well, for the sinners and not the righteous. Jesus never countenanced evil, but he did stand ready to forgive it. Somehow, he gained the reputation as a lover of sinners, a reputation that his followers are in danger of losing today. As Dorothy Day put it, "I really only love God as much as I love the person I love the least."

—

My book gives a detailed account of my friendship with Mel White. I won't reproduce it here, and I must admit I thought long and hard about including the story in my book. In the end, though, I felt it expressed much of what I have learned personally about grace. I hope that in your group, you use this as a case study in grace, responding to it honestly but without letting the conversation drift into a debate on the particular issue of homosexuality. That was not my point at all.

I learned an important insight into "different" people from Mel White's parents. They were interviewed on network television, along with Mel, his wife, and his friends. At one point, the TV interviewer asked Mel's parents on-camera, "You know what other Christians are saying about your son. They say he's an abomination. What do you think about that?"

"Well," the mother answered in a sweet, quavery voice, "he may be an abomination, but he's still our pride and joy."

That line has stayed with me because I came to see it as a heartrending definition of grace. I came to see that Mel White's mother expressed how God views every one of us. In some ways we are all abominations to God—*All have sinned and fall short of the glory of God*—and yet somehow, against all reason, God loves us anyhow. Grace declares that we are still God's pride and joy.

My friendship with Mel has taught me much about grace. On the surface the word may seem a shorthand expression for the fuzzy tolerance of liberalism: can't we all just get along? Grace is different, though. Traced back to its theological roots, it includes an element of self-sacrifice, a cost.

My study of Jesus' life convinces me that whatever barriers we must overcome in treating "different" people cannot compare to what a holy God—who dwelled in the Most Holy Place, and whose presence caused fire and smoke to belch from mountain-tops, bringing death to any unclean person who wandered near—overcame when he descended to join us on planet Earth.

We may be abominations, but we are still God's pride and joy. All of us in the church need "grace-healed eyes" to see the potential in others for the same grace that God has so lavishly bestowed on us. "To love a person," said Dostoevsky, "means to see him as God intended him to be."

The Music of Grace in God's Word

Read together the following passages from the Bible.

Romans 3:21–24
Colossians 4:5–6
1 Peter 4:7–11

The Harmony of Grace Around Me and Within
(25 Minutes)

If you are in a larger group, break into groups of four to six for this discussion time. Introduce yourselves to each other if necessary. Tell the group about yourself growing up. What made you feel like an oddball?

[Leader: We are covering a lot of material in this session. Consider ahead of time which questions you want to cover. If your schedule allows, you may want to consider spending two weeks on this session.]

1. What do you think of Will Campbell's summary of the Christian message: "We're all bastards but God loves us anyway"? Are you offended by the language? Have you ever felt anything like this—unworthy, illegitimate? How well does this statement paraphrase Romans 3:21–24?

In Will Campbell's experience, Thomas Coleman was one of the most obvious "bastards" around. When Campbell reckoned with the idea of God's love—and forgiveness— even for a murderer, he had uncovered the heart of the gospel. For some people, grappling with God's love for fundamentalist Christians is most difficult. For others, it is the thought of God's love for "politically correct" liberals, or wealthy conservatives, or feminists in the church. What types of people are the most challenging for you as you consider extending grace? Be sensitive to one another if you choose to discuss aloud.

What would you think of the idea of committing yourself to ministering to these kinds of people, as Campbell did to the Klansmen and racists?

2. Have you heard any teaching or opinions about why God
   restricted the eating of certain foods in Old Testament
   times? Briefly state what you have heard. Do you know
   any Jews who practice strict kosher?

Rabbi Jacob Neusner says, "If I had to say in a few words
what makes something unclean, it is something that, for
one reason or another, is abnormal." Men, women, and
animals with a variety of abnormalities were declared ceremonially unclean, and their access to God was restricted.
Does it trouble you to read of these Old Testament laws?
How would you feel, living in this kind of society today?
Imagine living as an "outcast" in this kind of society for
many years. Then a religious person who seems to be
from God comes and talks to you, touches you, eats at
your table, even though you are considered unclean. How
would you feel?

Review the stories of Jesus' compassion toward unclean
people. Many are discussed on pages 152–54 in the book,
or look them up in the Bible: the stories of men with leprosy, an adulterous woman who washed Jesus' feet with her
hair, tax collectors who hosted Jesus for dinner, a Roman
centurion with great faith, a Samaritan (half-breed) woman
at a well, a prodigal son, a Samaritan who saved a robbery
victim, a naked madman, a woman with a bleeding prob-

lem. Jesus set a new standard for godliness: We are called upon to extend God's mercy—to be conveyers of grace through the Spirit within us, not avoiders of contagion. Does this idea make you feel free to love? Is there a risk of losing sight of God's stand against sin?

3. Briefly consider how your biological father related to you when you were a child. Tell the group if you'd like.

Even if your father was not ideal, imagine that he was abundantly loving, quick to pull you onto his lap and hug you, always verbal in expressions of praise and adoration, never too busy for you and always ready to listen. Now think of God this way. Would speaking to God as "Daddy" seem natural? Would crying out to him feel safe?

What do Colossians 4:5–6 and 1 Peter 4:7–11 have to say about dispensing grace? Who do they tell us to be gracious toward? How do these commands reflect God's character?

Is there a place for Christians to take on the role of "moral exterminator"? Have you ever taken a strong moral stand regarding a particular issue? What was your motivation? How did you go about expressing your moral objection? How can a Christian take such a stand and express grace at the same time?

4. I told the story of my friendship with Mel White, a homosexual. How did you react to this story?

5. How do you feel about the response of the Christian protesters toward homosexuals that I describe in telling of the gay march on Washington, D.C. (pages 164–67 in the book)?

Are there any known homosexuals who worship in your church? If not, what do you think would happen if someone did come?

I mention the relative ease with which many churches love those divorced and those living together outside of marriage, while vehemently rejecting those who profess homosexuality. (Consider Matthew 5:21–22, 27–28, 31–32.) Do you think this is a fair comparison? Why or why not?

6. Does grace in the face of homosexuality, or any other moral issue, seem to you more like an excuse for tolerating liberalism? I learned in my friendship with Mel that offering grace isn't simply the easy way out. It involves a cost to me, a sacrifice, as well as a cost to Mel for his grace toward me. As you see it, what are the "risks" of grace?

See the quote by Helmut Thielicke on page 175 in the book. "Jesus did not *identify* the person with his sin, but rather saw in this sin something alien, something that really did not belong to him, something that merely chained and mastered him and from which he would free him and bring him back to his real self. Jesus was able to love men because he loved them right through the layer of mud." How close is your view of sinners to Jesus' view?

Do you have any prayer requests to share with the group?

God's Song of Grace to Me
(10–15 Minutes)

Listen to some music that celebrates love and grace, and then spend some time in silence with God. Pray as Jesus did, to your ever-loving parent—*Daddy, Abba*. Express your questions, ask for forgiveness, tell of your frustration, or simply groan in the presence of God, who knows and understands you. If you'd like, write your prayer in the space provided or in your journal.

Grace Notes

Listen together to a song by Kathy Troccoli, "Love One Another." It is found on her CD or cassette titled *Love and Mercy* (Reunion, 1997). The song is dedicated to Pastor Ray Highfield's His Touch Ministries, a Houston-based organization offering spiritual support to people with AIDS. More than forty Christian artists sing along with Kathy, including Sandi Patty, Amy Grant, Michael W. Smith, Babbie Mason, 4 Him, and Billy and Sarah Gaines. They speak of tearing down walls by God's grace. If you do not have access to Kathy Troccoli, sing together the praise song that goes

Spirit of the living God, fall afresh on me
Spirit of the living God, fall afresh on me
Melt me, mold me, fill me, use me
Spirit of the living God, fall afresh on me

Or find a hymnal and sing together "Jesus, Lover of My Soul."

Joining in the Song of Grace

- Pray this week about the fears you may have that are related to showing grace to people whom you have not been gracious toward in the past. Think about why you are afraid. Ask God to take your fears, put grace in their place, and begin a miraculous work.
- Consider contacting any of the following organizations, which minister to homosexuals and their families. Find out more about their ministry and how you or your church could extend the ministry to your community.

Exodus International. A Christian referral and resource network whose purpose is to proclaim that freedom from homosexuality is possible. P.O. Box 2121, San Rafael, CA 94912; phone 415-454-1017.

Desert Stream Ministries. Seeks to equip the body of Christ to effectively minister healing to the sexually and relationally broken, through the healing of individuals and the raising up of ministries in the context of the local church, based upon the biblical foundation of compassion, integrity, and dependence on God. P.O. Box 17635, Anaheim Hills, CA 92817-7635; phone 714-779-6899.

NARTH (National Association for Research and Therapy of Homosexuality). Seeks to make effective psychological therapy available to all homosexual men and women who seek change, as well as to open for public discussion all issues relating to homosexuality. 16542 Ventura Blvd., Suite 416, Encino, CA 91436; phone 818-789-4440.

Spatula Ministries. A ministry started by Christian author Barbara Johnson, committed to providing restoration to the family, especially those seeking to love a homosexual family member. A newsletter of support is available. P.O. Box 444, LaHabra, CA 90633-0444; phone 562-691-7369.

Background Music of Grace This Week
(Optional)

Day 1: Matthew 8:1–13
Day 2: Matthew 9:27–34
Day 3: Mark 5:21–34
Day 4: John 4:1–42
Day 5: Matthew 15:1–20

~

Week Nine

—

Loopholes

Chapter 14

To this point, I freely admit, I have presented a one-sided picture of grace. I have portrayed God as a lovesick father eager to forgive, and grace as a force potent enough to break the chains that bind us, and merciful enough to overcome deep differences between us. Depicting grace in such sweeping terms makes people nervous, and I concede that I have skated to the very edge of danger. I have done so because I believe the New Testament does too.

The potential for "grace abuse" was brought home to me forcefully in a conversation with a friend I'll call Daniel. One night I sat in a restaurant and listened as Daniel confided to me that he had decided to leave his wife after fifteen years of marriage. He had found someone younger and prettier, someone who "makes me feel alive, like I haven't felt in years." He and his wife had no strong incompatibilities. He simply wanted a change.

A Christian, Daniel knew well the personal and moral consequences of what he was about to do. His decision to leave would inflict permanent damage on his wife and three children. Even so, he said, the force pulling him toward the younger woman, like a powerful magnet, was too strong to resist.

I listened to Daniel's story with sadness and grief. Then, during the dessert course, he dropped the bombshell: "Actually, Philip, the reason I wanted to see you tonight was to ask you a question that's been bothering me. Do you think God can forgive something as awful as I am about to do?"

Daniel's question lay on the table like a live snake. I thought long and hard about the repercussions of grace. How can I dissuade my friend from committing a terrible mistake if he knows forgiveness lies just around the corner?

There is one "catch" to grace that I must now mention. In the words of C. S. Lewis, "St. Augustine says 'God gives where He finds empty hands.' A man whose hands are full of parcels can't receive a gift." Grace, in other words, must be received. Lewis explains that what I have termed "grace abuse" stems from a confusion of condoning and forgiving: "To condone an evil is simply to ignore it, to treat it as if it were good. But forgiveness needs to be accepted as well as offered if it is to be complete: and a man who admits no guilt can accept no forgiveness."

Here is what I told my friend Daniel, in a nutshell. "Can God forgive you? Of course. You know the Bible. God uses murderers and adulterers. For goodness' sake, a couple of scoundrels named Peter and Paul led the New Testament church. Forgiveness is *our* problem, not God's. What we have to go through to commit sin distances us from God —we change in the very act of rebellion—and there is no guarantee we will ever come back. You ask me about forgiveness now, but will you even want it later, especially if it involves repentance?"

Several months after our conversation, Daniel made his choice and left his family. I have yet to see evidence of repentance. Now he tends to rationalize his decision as a way of escaping an unhappy marriage. He has branded most of his former friends "too narrow-minded and judgmental," and looks instead for people who celebrate his newfound liberation. To me, though, Daniel does not seem very liberated. The price of "freedom" has meant turning his back on those who cared about him most. He also tells me God is not a part of his life right now. "Maybe later," he says.

God took a great risk by announcing forgiveness in advance, and the scandal of grace involves a transfer of that risk to us.

—

Twentieth-century theologian Dietrich Bonhoeffer coined the phrase "cheap grace" as a way of summarizing grace abuse. Every call to conversion, he insisted, includes a call to discipleship. As Dallas Willard puts it, we need to be equally concerned about the cost of *non*-discipleship.

In the book of Romans, Paul bores in on these very issues. Why be good if you know in advance you will be forgiven? He begins with a basic analogy that starkly contrasts death and life. "We died to sin; how can we live in it any longer?" he asks, incredulous. No Christian resurrected to new life should be pining for the grave. Sin has the stench of death about it. Why would anyone choose it?

Paul, a realist, recognized that even in Christians, sin keeps popping back to life, or else he would not have advised us in the same passage, "*Count* yourselves dead to sin" and "Do not let sin reign in your mortal body."

Paul's second analogy, human slavery, adds a new dimension to the discussion. "You used to be slaves to sin," he begins. Sin is a slave master that controls us whether we like it or not. Paradoxically, a headlong pursuit of freedom often turns into bondage. For many, sin feels like a kind of slavery.

In yet a third illustration, Paul likens the spiritual life to marriage. The intensity of feeling we have for the one person we choose to spend life with mirrors the passion God feels toward us, and God wants his passion returned in kind.

That reality helps me understand Paul's gruff "God forbid!" response to the question "Shall we go on sinning that grace may increase?" Would a groom on his wedding night ask his bride whether he could have an affair now and then so she would have the chance to forgive him?

To such a Don Juan the only reasonable response is a slap in the face and a "God forbid!" Obviously, he does not understand the first thing about love. Indeed, God wants something more intimate than the closest relationship on earth, the lifetime bond between a man and a woman. What God wants is not a good performance, but my heart.

If I had to summarize the primary New Testament motivation for "being good" in one word, I would choose *gratitude*. If we comprehend what Christ has done for us, then surely out of gratitude we will strive to live "worthy" of such great love. A person who truly loves God will be inclined to please God, which is why Jesus and Paul both summed up the entire law in the simple command, "Love God."

The Music of Grace in God's Word

Read together the following passage from the Bible.

Romans 6

The Harmony of Grace Around Me and Within
(25 Minutes)

If you are in a larger group, break into groups of four to six for this discussion time. Introduce yourselves to each other if necessary. Tell the group about one of the first paying jobs you held growing up. What wages did you receive?

1. Consider the story of the prisoner at the beginning of chapter 14 in the book. Wanting to die, he considered suicide, which he believed would send him straight to hell. Instead, the prisoner murdered a fellow inmate, believing he would have the chance to confess to a priest and receive forgiveness before being executed. Consider also the story of my friend Daniel, who questioned whether God would forgive his divorcing his wife. How would you have answered Daniel?

Have you ever made a conscious decision to sin, with the thought of God's future forgiveness in mind? What thoughts went through your head? Share the details of the sin only as you desire.

If you went ahead and committed the sin, did you later desire forgiveness? How long did it take for you to want forgiveness? What kind of thought process did you go through to get to this point? Why is it so difficult for us to admit fault, confess sin, and repent?

2. Turn to the story of the adulterous woman in John 8:1–11. Whom do you more closely resemble—the woman or the accusers? Do you see sin more quickly in another or in yourself? Do you more often deny or rationalize away your own sin or confess it?

Have you known anyone who has suffered an addiction to alcohol or to another substance or behavior? What did it take for this person to acknowledge the problem and seek help?

3. What role has discipleship—the act of following and learning from Jesus—played in your life? In what ways have you consciously tried to attain holiness because of your love for God? What obstacles have you run into?

4. Which of the following rationalizations of sin that Paul addresses in Romans 6–7 hits closest to home in your life?

   • If grace increases as sin increases, then why not sin extravagantly so God can give more grace? God loves being gracious, so I'll help him out.
   • I'm not under law but under grace. It doesn't matter if I sin—God has given me freedom.
   • Why be good, if I know I am saved? How good do I really have to be?
   • I may be sinning now, but does it really matter, since God will forgive me anyway?

   What is Paul's—or God's—response to the rationalization you chose?

   In your own experience, which is a more powerful motive for behavior—fear of punishment, or a desire to please someone you love? Does the Bible use both motivations?

Have you ever felt like Nancy Mairs (see pages 190–91 in the book), who for many years followed the "God of the Gotcha"—one who set her up for trespass by forbidding behaviors he clearly expected her to commit? How have you come to know the God who, in Mairs' words, "asks for the single act that will make transgression impossible: love"? Or are you still looking for this God?

Do you have any prayer needs to express to the group?

God's Song of Grace to Me
(10–15 Minutes)

Listen to music about grace, and then spend some time in silence with God. Sit with your hands open, palms up, in a gesture of humility, as a sinner in need of God's grace. Pray or simply sit in God's presence, expressing your need through this act. After spending several minutes in this posture with God, you may want to write in your journal or in the space provided.

Grace Notes

Listen together to a song titled "God of Grace and God of Glory" by classical guitarist Christopher Parkening. He is a world-renowned guitarist and a Christian. This song is found on his CD or cassette titled *Simple Gifts* (Angel, 1982). Or listen to "Not under Law" by the Scripture Memory Singers on their CD or cassette titled *Songs of Hope and Encouragement* (Hosanna Integrity, 1996). This song puts to music parts of Romans 6.

If you do not have access to Christopher Parkening or Scripture Memory Singers, find a hymnal and sing together "O Jesus, I Have Promised." Sing along with a piano, guitar, or *a capella*.

Joining in the Song of Grace

- This week monitor your thoughts as you consider engaging in "everyday" sin such as gossip, telling a lie, coveting, lusting, slandering, or being unkind. What goes through your mind in the moments before you commit or refrain from committing the sin?
- This week spend some time in prayer, beginning in an attitude of humility, with hands open, desiring God's grace. Pray that God would give you eyes to see yourself honestly, in your own sin and need. Pray also for growth in your love relationship with your Savior.

Background Music of Grace This Week
(Optional)

Read the following Bible passages and reflections this week in your quiet moments. Meditate on these readings as your time allows.

Day 1: James 1
Day 2: James 2
Day 3: James 3
Day 4: James 4
Day 5: James 5

Before writing this chapter, I slowly read the entire New Testament, marking on a yellow legal pad every passage that encouraged believers to be "good" or "holy" or to do any sort of good works. I tried to peer beneath the straightforward commands—"steal no more; stop gossiping"—to the underlying motive. To what was Jesus, Paul, James, John, Jude, or Peter appealing? I filled many pages of my legal pad with notes and went over them repeatedly in search of trends.

It became clear to me that the New Testament presents the Christian life as a journey along which believers can be found at many different places. For the sake of convenience, I divided the stages into three rough groupings: child, adult, and parent. I started marking in the margins which of these stages the author was addressing.

A surprising number of the passages I recorded from the New Testament earned a *C* in the margin for childlike appeal. Jesus did not hesitate to threaten dire punishment for the disobedient or promise lavish rewards to the obedient. In his one book, the apostle James lectures like a schoolmarm. For his part, Paul warned the Thessalonians of coming judgment, and even his grace-saturated letter of Galatians contains the warning, "Do not be deceived: God cannot be mocked. A man reaps what he sows." Paul's "childlike" admonitions usually come with a large dose of exasperation. "Don't you know? ... Don't you realize?" he sputters, frustrated that people called by God to be saints are instead squabbling over matters like eating meat and circumcision. He gives pep talks, much like a father who urges his child to eat spinach or practice the piano "for your own good."

If I had to summarize the "adult appeals" in one word, it would be *gratitude*. When writing letters to mature believers, Paul always begins with a summary of the riches we possess in Christ. If we grasp some notion of the wonderful things Christ has done for us, then surely we will respond with a sense of gratitude, striving to live a life "worthy" of such great love. We will please him as a lover pleases the beloved, not out of compulsion but out of desire. We will strive for holiness not to make God love us but because he does. As Paul told Titus, it is the grace of God that "teaches us to say 'No' to ungodliness and worldly passions, and to live self-controlled, upright and godly lives."

Paul's letters shift into a more relaxed tone when he addresses people who are earnestly striving to please God, as opposed to those who are playing childish games with other Christians. Contentious issues will always arise, but we can deal with them as adults. In Paul's day the issues involved such matters as vegetarianism, pagan festival days, meat sacrificed to idols, circumcision, and the worship of angels. (Remember, just a generation ago the church was debating the morality of mustaches, roller-skating, jazz, interracial dating, and coed swimming.)

In Romans and in 1 Corinthians, Paul uses the term "weaker brother" to describe an immature, newborn Christian too insecure to let go of a clinging dependence on rules. He uses "strong" to refer to Christians, like himself, who feel free from petty rules and restrictions and take their guidance on such matters directly from the Holy Spirit. Paul insisted on his freedom, as the fierce words of Galatians make clear. Yet he never abused it. Though he personally had no qualms about eating meat and observing holidays, as a mature Christian (read "adult"), he modified his behavior for the sake of weaker, immature Christians. "Discipleship," says Clifford Williams, "simply means the life which springs from grace."

A final set of motives appeals to what I call "parental" instincts. Gradually, gently, Paul and the other apostles press their flock to move beyond self-fulfillment. Like any human parent, the mature Christian lives not for himself or herself but for the sake of others.

Christians are urged to avoid lawsuits for the sake of the watching world. Peter says that husbands can be won to Christ by the behavior of their wives. We are called to be not merely receptacles of grace but dispensers as well. "It is for freedom that Christ has set us free," trumpets Galatians. "But," Paul adds in the same chapter, "do not use your freedom to indulge the sinful nature; rather, serve one another in love."

The parental role of reproduction and nurturing is a high calling. Jesus told his followers to "let your light shine before men, that they may see your good deeds and praise your Father in heaven." Paul described the Corinthians as "our letter, written on our hearts, known and read by everybody."

Persistently the New Testament presses us upward to the higher motives of morality. A child wants to know what she can get away with; an adult understands that boundaries exist for his own good; a parent voluntarily sacrifices her own freedom for the sake of others.

Week Ten

Grace Avoidance

Chapter 15

I have had many close-up encounters with legalism. I came out of a Southern fundamentalist culture that frowned on coed swimming, wearing shorts, jewelry or makeup, dancing, bowling, and reading the Sunday newspaper. Alcohol was a sin of a different order, with the sulfurous stench of hellfire about it.

Later I attended a Bible college where, in an era of miniskirts, deans legislated a skirt length below the knee. Male students had their own rules, including a restriction against hair covering the ears and a ban on facial hair. Dating was strictly regulated. The college also attempted to monitor a student's relationship with God. Early each morning a bell rang, summoning us to rise and have personal devotions. If caught sleeping in, we would have to read and write a report on a Christian book.

What bothers me most, in retrospect, was the Bible college's attempt to relate all their rules to God's law. In chapel services, the deans and professors would painstakingly try to ground each rule in biblical principles. I could find not one word in the Bible about rock music, skirt lengths, or cigarette smoking, yet authorities in that school made a determined effort to present all these rules as part of the gospel. The subculture got muddled with the message.

I now recognize that the severity of fundamentalism may have kept me out of trouble. Strict legalism pulls in the bounds of deviance: we might sneak off to a bowling alley, but would never think of touching liquor or—horrors!—drugs. I have little resentment against these particular rules but much resentment against the way they were presented. I had the constant, pounding sense that following an external code of behavior was the way to please God—more, to make God love me. It has taken me years to distill the gospel out of the subculture in which I first encountered it. Sadly, many of my friends gave up on the effort, never getting to Jesus because the pettiness of the church blocked the way.

As I study the life of Jesus, one fact consistently surprises me: the group that made Jesus angriest was the group that, externally at least, he most resembled—the Pharisees. Yet Jesus singled out the Pharisees for his strongest attacks. "Snakes!" he called them. "Brood of vipers! Fools! Hypocrites! Blind guides! Whitewashed tombs!"

The Pharisees had much in common with those whom the press might call Bible-belt fundamentalists today. They devoted their lives to following God and obeyed every minute law in the Torah. Jesus' fierce denunciations of the Pharisees show how seriously he viewed the toxic threat of legalism.

Overall, Jesus condemned the legalists' emphasis on *externals*. Expressions of love for God had, over time, evolved into ways of impressing others. Over time, the spirit of law-keeping stiffens into *extremism*. I know of no legalism that does not seek to enlarge its domain of intolerance.

In some Christian groups today, extremism is on the rise. Where legalism takes root, the prickly thorns of extremism eventually branch out. Legalism is a subtle danger because no one thinks of himself as a legalist. My own rules seem necessary; other people's rules seem excessively strict.

Jesus faulted the Pharisees less for their extremism than for their focus on *trivialities* over more weighty matters. The same teachers who tithed their kitchen spices had little to say about the injustice and oppression in Palestine. When Jesus healed a person on the Sabbath, his critics seemed far more concerned about protocol than about the sick person.

What sobers me is that contemporary Christians may someday be judged just as harshly. What trivialities do we obsess over, and what weighty matters of the law—justice, mercy, faithfulness—might we be missing? Does God care more about nose rings or about urban decay? Grunge music or world hunger? Worship styles or a culture of violence?

Jesus' critique centered on what legalism does to the law-keeper: it fosters feelings of *pride* and *competition*. Instead of getting on with the task of creating a just society that would shine as a light to the Gentiles, the Pharisees narrowed their vision and began competing with each other. Caught up in trying to impress each other with spiritual calisthenics, they lost contact with the real enemy, as well as with the rest of the world.

Henri Nouwen writes,

> The spiritual games we play, many of which begin with the best of motives, can perversely lead us away from God, because they lead us away from grace. Repentance, not proper behavior or even holiness, is the doorway to grace.

Legalism fails miserably at the one thing it is supposed to do: encourage obedience. In a strange twist, a system of strict laws actually puts new ideas of lawbreaking in a person's mind. For those who do not rebel, but rather strive sincerely to keep the rules, legalism sets another trap. The feelings of failure may cause long-lasting scars of shame. As a young monk, Martin Luther would spend as long as six hours racking his brain to confess the sins he might have committed the previous day!

One final complaint against legalism burdens me in a deeply personal way. I have referred to friends who rejected the Christian faith in large part because of the church's petty legalism. How many strict Christian families have watched as a child abandons faith, casting aside rules and beliefs as easily as one casts aside a too-small jacket? Legalism makes apostasy easy.

I have written about legalism partly because of my own bruising encounters with it and partly because I believe it represents such a powerful temptation to the church. Legalism stands like a stripper on the sidelines of faith, seducing us toward an easier way. It teases, promising some of the benefits of faith but unable to deliver what matters most. As Paul wrote to the legalists of his day, "For the kingdom of God is not a matter of eating and drinking, but of righteousness, peace and joy in the Holy Spirit."

At first glance legalism seems hard, but actually freedom in Christ is the harder way. It is relatively easy not to murder, hard to reach out in love; easy to avoid a neighbor's bed, hard to keep a marriage alive; easy to pay taxes, hard to serve the poor. When living in freedom, I must remain open to the Spirit for guidance. I am more aware of what I have neglected than what I have achieved. I cannot hide behind a mask of behavior, like the hypocrites, nor can I hide behind facile comparisons with other Christians.

Jesus proclaimed unmistakably that God's law is so perfect and absolute that no one can achieve righteousness. Yet God's grace is so great that we do not have to. By striving to prove how much they deserve God's love, legalists miss the whole point of the gospel, that it is a gift from God to people who don't deserve it. The solution to sin is not to impose an ever-stricter code of behavior. It is to know God.

The Music of Grace in God's Word

Read together the following passage from the Bible.

Matthew 23

The Harmony of Grace Around Me and Within
(25 Minutes)

If you are in a larger group, break into groups of four to six for this discussion time. Introduce yourselves to each other if necessary. Tell the group about your least-favorite household chore. Washing the dishes? Cleaning the bathroom? Taking out the garbage? Cleaning up after your pet?

1. Did you encounter legalism growing up? As an adult? What kind of legalism? How did you respond to it? Did it affect you negatively? Positively? Are there any lasting effects?

2. Are you a person who more naturally falls into legalism or rebellion? Why do you think you lean more in this direction?

3. Concerning legalism, which of the following comes closest to describing you? Explain to the group, knowing we will all fall into some of these tendencies at times.

- A legalistic emphasis on externals: I sometimes fall into the desire to impress others with my actions. I want people to feel I'm a deeply spiritual person.
- A legalistic extremism: Better safe than sorry is how I sometimes feel. Like they say, "If you give an inch, they'll take a mile." I tend to want more rules so I and others don't stray from God.
- A legalistic emphasis on trivialities: I care about the weighty matters, like justice and faithfulness, but feel overwhelmed by them. It's easier to control the smaller things, like dress and music. Sometimes I feel this is a manageable way of doing my part.
- An urge to rebel due to legalism: I feel certain religious practices are important, but struggle with a spirit of rebellion against these practices.
- A legalistic sense of failure: I struggle with feeling that I'm constantly failing God or have failed him in a big way in the past.

- Alienation from God due to legalism: I struggle with relating to God due to the legalism in my past.

4. My Southern church had much to say about hairstyle, jewelry, and rock music but not a word about racial injustice and the plight of blacks in the South. Would you say that people in your church are more concerned with trivialities or the weightier matters of the gospel (caring for the poor and needy, both nearby and far away; sharing the gospel; worshiping God)? How can you help move the focus to what matters most?

5. Instead of getting on with the task of creating a just society that would shine as a light to the Gentiles, the Pharisees narrowed their vision and began competing with each other. Caught up in trying to impress each other with spiritual calisthenics, they lost contact with the real enemy, as well as with the rest of the world.

   Have you ever fallen into a sort of spiritual calisthenics within a Christian community, in which you became concerned with meeting the approval of or competing with the Christians in your group rather than reaching out to the world around you? How did this happen? What made you realize it was wrong?

6. Read the quote by Henri Nouwen on pages 205–6 in the book. Nouwen speaks of his constant efforts to avoid sin. He says, "There came a seriousness, a moralistic intensity—and even a touch of fanaticism—that made it

increasingly difficult to feel at home in my Father's house. I became less free, less spontaneous, less playful . . ." Have you ever experienced similar feelings in your efforts to please God? How did you handle these feelings?

7. Do you agree that legalism might actually be easier than true freedom in Christ? Why? What does freedom in Christ mean for your life? For your lifestyle? For your marriage? For your role as a parent? For your relationship with non-Christians? For your relationship with God?

Do you have any prayer needs to share with the group?

God's Song of Grace to Me
(10–15 Minutes)

Listen to some music about grace, and then spend some time with God in silent prayer or meditation. You may want to add on to the prayer below in the space provided or in your journal.

Grace Notes

Listen together to the praise song "Only by Grace." It is found on the CD or cassette by Petra titled *Petra Praise 2* (Word, 1997), in the song titled "Medley." If you do not have access to Petra, sing the praise song along with guitar, piano, or *a capella,* if you know the tune. The words read,

> Only by grace can we enter, only by grace can we stand
> Not by our human endeavors, but by the blood of the lamb.
> Lord, if you marked our transgressions who could stand,
> But by your grace we are saved by the blood of the Lamb.

If you don't know this praise song, find the words to "O for a Thousand Tongues" in a hymnal and sing it together.

———

Dear God, I want to follow you rightly. More than anything, I want to live out the freedom you've given me. But I'm not always sure how to do that. I fall into old patterns. I get confused by the voices around me. Even more confusing are the voices inside. I can plug my ears and, like a child, sing a song to drown out the clamor, but then I miss hearing you. Give me an ear for your voice. Teach me the rhythm of your freedom. Set me dancing to the music of your Spirit. . . .

Joining in the Song of Grace

- This week think about the areas in which you've fallen into legalism in the past and maybe still fall sometimes. Do you place your own legalistic expectations on others and judge them, inwardly or outwardly, for not adhering to your standard?

- This week begin the conscious practice of discernment. When an "I should" voice comes to mind, make it a matter of prayer. Pray before acting. Ask God to tell you his perspective. Open yourself to hearing answers you may not have expected. You may want to record in a journal your prayers and God's answers as he gradually gives them.

Background Music of Grace This Week
(Optional)

Read the following Bible passages and additional reading this week in your quiet moments. Reflect on these readings as your time allows.

Day 1: Galatians 1
Day 2: Galatians 2
Day 3: Galatians 3:1–25
Day 4: Galatians 3:26–4:31
Day 5: Galatians 5–6

A few years ago I attended a conference at a place called New Harmony, the restored site of a century-old Utopian community. As I ran my fingers over the fine workmanship of the buildings and read the plaques describing the daily lives of the true believers, I marveled at the energy that drove this movement, one of the dozens spawned by American idealism and religious fervor.

Many varieties of perfectionism have grown on American soil: the offshoots of the Second Great Awakening, the Victorious Life movement, the communes of the Jesus movement. It struck me, though, that in recent times the urge to achieve perfection has nearly disappeared. Nowadays we tilt in the opposite direction, toward a kind of anti-Utopianism. The recovery movement, for example, hinges on a person's self-confessed *inability* to be perfect.

I prefer this modern trend. I find it much easier to believe in human fallibility than perfectibility, and I have cast my lot with a gospel based on grace. Yet in New Harmony, Indiana, I felt an unaccountable nostalgia for the Utopians: all those solemn figures in black clothes breaking rocks in the fields, devising ever-stricter rules in an attempt to rein in lust and greed, striving to fulfill the lofty commands of the New Testament. The names they left behind tug at the heart: New Harmony, Peace Dale, New Hope, New Haven.

Yet most Utopian communities—like the one I was standing in—survive only as museums. Perfectionism keeps running aground on the barrier reef of original sin. High ideals paradoxically lead to despair and defeatism. Despite all good efforts, human beings don't achieve a state of sinlessness, and in the end they often blame themselves (a blame encouraged by their leaders: "If it is not working, there must be something wrong with you.").

Still, I admit that I sometimes feel a nostalgia, even longing, for the quest itself. How can we uphold the ideal of holiness, the proper striving for life on the highest plane, while avoiding the consequences of disillusionment, pettiness, abuse of authority, spiritual pride, and exclusivism?

Or, to ask the opposite question, how can we moderns who emphasize community support (never judgment), honesty, and introspection keep from aiming too low? An individualistic society, America stands in constant danger of freedom abuse; its churches are in danger of grace abuse.

It was with these questions in mind that I read through the Epistles, charting the motives they appealed to. I read them in a different order than usual. First I read Galatians, with its magnificent charter of Christian liberty, and its fiery pronouncements against petty legalism. Next I turned to James, that "right strawy epistle" that stuck in Martin Luther's throat. I read Ephesians and then 1 Corinthians, Romans and then 1 Timothy, Colossians and then 1 Peter. In every epistle, without exception, I found both messages: the high ideals of holiness, and also the safety net of grace reminding us that salvation does not depend on our meeting those ideals. I will not attempt to resolve the tension between grace and works, because the New Testament does not. We must not try to solve the contradiction by reducing the force of either grace or morality. Grace presents a "Yes and," not a "Yes but."

Ephesians pulls the two strands neatly together: "For it is by *grace you have been saved,* through faith—and this not from yourselves, it is the gift of God—not by works, so that no one can boast. For we are God's workmanship, created in Christ Jesus *to do good works,* which God prepared in advance for us to do" (emphasis mine). Philippians expresses the same dialectic: "*Work out your salvation* with fear and trembling, for it is *God who works in you* to will and to act according to his good purpose" (emphasis mine). First Peter adds, "Live as free men, but do not use your freedom as a cover-up for evil; live as servants of God."

I take some comfort in the fact that the church in the first century was already on a seesaw, tilting now toward perfectionist legalism and now toward raucous freedom. James wrote to one extreme; Paul often addressed the other. Each letter has a strong correcting emphasis, but all stress the dual message of the gospel. The church should be both: a people who strive toward holiness and yet relax in grace, a people who condemn themselves but not others, a people who depend on God and not themselves.

Morality, Politics, and Grace

Chapters 16 and 17

~

I had a rude introduction to contemporary culture wars when I visited the White House during Bill Clinton's first term, as part of a group of twelve evangelicals. The President was convening us primarily because of his low standing among evangelical Christians. Mr. Clinton addressed some of those concerns in his opening remarks, confessing, "Sometimes I feel like a spiritual orphan."

As a lifelong Southern Baptist, he was finding it difficult to locate a Christian community in Washington, D.C.—"the most secular city I've ever lived in." The conservative Christian community had disassociated itself from him. When the President jogged through the streets of Washington he saw bumper stickers like this one: "A vote for Bill Clinton is a sin against God."

The President had not experienced much grace from Christians. "I've been in politics long enough to expect criticism and hostility," the President told us. "But I was unprepared for the *hatred* I get from Christians. Why do Christians hate so much?"

Of course, everyone in the Lincoln Dining Room that morning knew why the President stirred up such animosity among Christians. His policies on abortion and homosexual rights, in particular, along with reports of his own moral failings, made it difficult for many Christians to take seriously his profession of faith.

I wrote an article about that breakfast, and a few months later another invitation came from the White House, this time offering an exclusive magazine interview with the President. My article that resulted, "The Riddle of Bill Clinton's Faith," reported his views and also explored a question raised by a friend of mine. Can Bill Clinton possibly be sincere about his faith, holding the views that he does? I had done much research, including conversations with his friends and associates from childhood, and the evidence seemed clear: Clinton's faith was not posturing for political expediency but an integral part of who he was. In fact, I found it almost impossible to understand the Clintons apart from their religious faith.

I wrote what I thought was a balanced account of President Clinton and his faith, giving considerable space to the issue of abortion. I was totally unprepared for the firestorm of reaction.

"You say Clinton has biblical knowledge," said one; "well, so does the Devil! You got snowed." Many writers contended that evangelicals should never have met with the President. Six drew parallels with Adolf Hitler, who cynically used pastors for his own purposes. Several more likened us to the church browbeaten by Stalin. Others recalled biblical scenes of confrontation: John the Baptist and Herod, Elijah and Ahab, Nathan and David. Why hadn't I acted more like a prophet, shaking my finger in the President's face?

Less than ten percent of the letters had positive things to say, and the vicious tone of personal attack caught me off guard. In twenty-five years of journalism I have received my share of mixed reviews. Even so, as I read through stacks of vituperative letters I got a strong sense for why the world does not automatically associate the word "grace" with evangelical Christians.

As the apostle Paul did in his writings, I have presented grace as a wonderful force that can break the chains of ungrace binding nations, tribes, and families. It conveys the best news possible, that the God of the universe loves us—news so good it bears the scent of scandal. But my task is not over. The time has come to return to a practical question: If grace is so amazing, why don't Christians show more of it?

How is it that Christians called to dispense the aroma of grace instead emit the noxious fumes of ungrace? In the United States in the 1990s, one answer to that question springs readily to mind. The church has allowed itself to get so swept up in political issues that it plays by the rules of power, which are rules of ungrace. In no other arena is the church at greater risk of losing its calling than in the public square.

I fully support the right, and indeed the responsibility, of Christians to get involved politically. As they do so, some Christians are acting ungraciously out of fear. We feel under attack in schools, in courts, and sometimes in Congress. Meanwhile we see around us the kind of moral change that marks society's decay. But, as Jesus pointed out to the Pharisees, a concern for moral values alone is not nearly enough. Moralism apart from grace solves little.

When I ask my airplane seatmates, "What comes to mind when I say the words 'evangelical Christian'?" they usually respond in political terms. Yet the gospel of Jesus was not primarily a political platform. In all the talk of voting blocs and culture wars, the message of grace—the main distinctive Christians have to offer—tends to fall aside. It is difficult, if not impossible, to communicate the message of grace from the corridors of power.

I think back to the life of Jesus, who attracted as if by reverse magnetism the most unsavory of characters, the moral outcasts. He came for the sinners, not the righteous. And when he was arrested it was not the notorious sinners of Palestine, but the moralists, who called for his death.

"Be careful," warned Nietzsche, "lest in fighting the dragon you become the dragon."

Jesus came to found a new kind of kingdom that could coexist in Jerusalem and also spread into Judea, Samaria, and the uttermost parts of the earth. In a parable he warned that those farmers who concentrate on pulling up weeds (his image for "sons of the evil one") may destroy the wheat along with the weeds. Leave matters of judgment to the one true Judge, Jesus advised.

When I went to the White House to visit President Clinton, I knew well that his reputation among conservative Christians hinged on two issues: abortion and homosexual rights. I agree fully that these are important moral issues which Christians must address. But when I went through the New Testament I could find very little related to either one. Both practices existed then, in a different and more egregious form. Roman citizens did not rely principally on abortion for birth control. The women bore their babies, then abandoned them by the side of the road for wild animals or vultures. Likewise, Romans and Greeks also practiced a form of same-gender sex: older men commonly used young boys as their sex slaves, in pederasty.

Thus in Jesus' and Paul's day both these moral issues asserted themselves in ways that today would be criminal in any civilized country on earth. Jesus and Paul doubtless knew of these deplorable practices. And yet Jesus said nothing about either one, and Paul made only a few references to cross-gender sex. Both concentrated not on the pagan kingdom around them but on the alternative kingdom of God.

For this reason, I wonder about the enormous energy being devoted these days to restoring morality to the United States. Are we concentrating more on the kingdom of this world than on the kingdom that is not of this world? How will we feel if historians of the future look back on the evangelical church of the 1990s and declare, "They fought bravely on the moral fronts of abortion and homosexual rights," while at the same time reporting that we did little to fulfill the Great Commission, and we did little to spread the aroma of grace in the world?

The Music of Grace in God's Word

Read together the following passage from the Bible.

Matthew 13:24–30, 36–43

~

The Harmony of Grace Around Me and Within
(25 Minutes)

If you are in a larger group, break into groups of four to six for this discussion time. Introduce yourselves if necessary and tell the group about one of the most beautiful gardens you have seen. Where is the garden? Who tends it?

1. Review together the story (in chapter 16 in the book) of my friend, Big Harold, who moved his family to South Africa to live under white-dominated rule, where morality was enforced. Several years after moving, Big Harold was sent to jail for pornography and harassment. Even after his prison experience, he continued to focus on morality rather than grace.

   Can you identify with anything about Big Harold? Have you ever wanted to flee the country or in some other way shelter yourself and your family from the immorality around you? Have you ever responded to moral failure—your own or others'—with a desire to work even harder at enforcing morality? Explain. How *should* Harold have responded?

2. Can you think of a situation in our society in which, in your own thinking, enforcing morality seems right, even at the expense of dispensing grace? Maybe in laws regarding smoking? Drugs? Gun control? Parents' rules for teenagers and dating?

3. What is your reaction to my experience with President Bill Clinton? If a government leader holds positions that you believe to be unbiblical, what do you feel is the biblical way to speak to and about that leader? What is the biblical way to oppose policies you feel are unbiblical? To what extent

are Christians responsible for determining whether a leader is truly a follower of Christ or not?

If you had five minutes to address the President, what would you say?

4. Andy Rooney says he is against abortion, yet he prefers spending time with pro-choice rather than pro-life people. Does that imply that in the world's eyes Christians must either uphold morals or grace but can't do both? What do you think—can Christians uphold moral values in a secular society while at the same time conveying a spirit of grace?

5. Think about the people you know who aren't followers of Jesus. If you asked them the question, "What comes to mind when I say the words 'evangelical Christian'?" what do you think they would say? Try it this week on a stranger or acquaintance.

What would you *like* them to say?

6. I see the confusion of politics and religion as one of the greatest barriers to grace. C. S. Lewis once said that almost all crimes of Christian history have come about when religion was confused with politics. Politics, which always runs by the rules of ungrace, allures us to trade away grace for power, a temptation the church has often been unable to resist.

In a democracy, we should be politically involved because, after all, we are the government. How has your own political involvement brought about challenges to you as a Christian? Have you ever been involved in local politics? Maybe the PTA or school board? Have you been involved in local or national issues such as abortion, gay rights, pornography on the Internet, welfare reform, gun control, foreign aid, or others? Has your church ever become involved politically?

6. Look again at the parable of the wheat and weeds in Matthew 13. Look at the parable and at the explanation. Envision yourself, a follower of Jesus, as wheat amid weeds in a vast field. Notice the language Jesus used in the explanation of the parable. He talks of sin and evil and burning fire. If Jesus speaks so strongly about those whom the weeds represent, he must take seriously the wrongs we encounter. Notice also that the wheat survives until the harvest, despite the difficulties.

Take a moment as a small group or as a large group to lay hands on one another and pray for the strength to live as wheat among weeds in the world. Pray that our lives would not focus so much on containing the weeds that in an attempt to pull them, we also destroy the growth of the gospel. Pray for love and humility, that we may shine for God's kingdom here on earth as we wait eagerly for Jesus' return.

Do you have any prayer needs you would like to express to the group?

God's Song of Grace to Me
(10–15 Minutes)

Listen together to a song about grace, and then spend some time in silence with God. You may want to pray for the Spirit's direction in your heart as you reflect on today's discussion. Or you may want to sit with your hands opened and eyes closed, praying a simple prayer for God's grace-filled Being to inhabit you. If you choose to write a prayer or take notes, you can use the space provided or write in your journal.

Grace Notes

Listen together to the song "Gather at the River" by Point of Grace, on their CD or cassette titled *The Whole Truth.* They sing of gathering at the river of forgiveness, reaching out to those whom Jesus called us to love. If you don't have access to Point of Grace, find a hymnal and sing together the song "Come, Thou Fount." Or sing the song "They'll Know We Are Christians by Our Love." Sing with guitar, piano, or *a capella*.

Joining in the Song of Grace

- This week focus on a moral issue that especially concerns you. What emotions have filled your thinking regarding this issue? What has been your approach to encouraging what you believe to be biblical behavior? How have you spoken about this issue to both Christians and non-Christians? What actions have you taken to support your viewpoint? How have you prayed about this issue? As you think, pray that God would help you to look honestly at yourself.

- After considering these questions for a few days, pray during the next days for God to develop more fully within you his own love of both holiness and grace. Pray that God would guide your thoughts, words, and actions as you continue in your concern over this issue. Pray also about the issue itself. You may want to pray on your knees, seeking an attitude of submission, surrender, and supplication.

- Find someone who is actively involved in the political arena or actively working for a political cause. Talk with them about the ideas discussed in today's session. Ask for their thoughts. Be loving and sensitive, careful not to criticize. Through loving, respect-filled conversation, we can all continue to learn and grow.

Background Music of Grace This Week
(Optional)

Use the following Bible passages in your quiet moments this week as you reflect on God's grace. Use these readings as your time allows.

Day 1: Matthew 13:1–23
Day 2: Matthew 13:31–35, 44–46
Day 3: Matthew 13:47–52
Day 4: Matthew 5:13–16
Day 5: Matthew 10:5–42

Week Twelve

Serpent Wisdom

Chapter 18

⁓

When I grew up in the 1950s, the school principal began each day with a prayer read over the intercom system. In school we pledged allegiance to a nation "under God," and in Sunday school we pledged allegiance to both the American and the Christian flags. It never occurred to me that America might one day present Christians with a new challenge: how to "grace" a society increasingly hostile to them.

Until recently American history—the official version, at least—presented a waltz between two dancing partners, church and state. Our founders thought religious faith essential for a democracy to work. For most of our history, even the Supreme Court echoed the Christian consensus.

Nowadays few people confuse church and state in the United States, and the change occurred with such breathtaking speed that anyone born in the last thirty years may wonder what Christian consensus I am talking about. Much of the outrage of the religious right stems from the swiftness of this cultural shift.

The culture war is under way. Ironically, every year the church in the United States draws closer and closer to the situation faced by the New Testament church: an embattled minority living in a pluralistic, pagan society. Christians in places like Sri Lanka, Tibet, Sudan, and Saudi Arabia have faced open hostility from their governments for years. But in the United States, with a history so congenial to the faith, we don't like it.

How can Christians dispense grace in a society that seems to be veering away from God? The Bible offers many different models of response. Elijah hid out in caves and made lightning raids on Ahab's pagan regime; his contemporary Obadiah worked within the system, running Ahab's palace while sheltering God's true prophets on the side. Esther and Daniel were employed by heathen empires; Jonah called down judgment on another. Jesus submitted to the judgment of a Roman governor; Paul appealed his case all the way to Caesar.

To complicate matters, the Bible gives no direct advice for citizens of a democracy. When some form of Christian consensus held sway in the United States, these issues were less urgent. Now all of us who love our faith and also our nation must decide how best to express that care. I offer three preliminary conclusions that ought to apply no matter what the future brings.

First, as should be clear by now, I believe that dispensing God's grace is the Christian's main contribution. As Gordon Mac-Donald said, the world can do anything the church can do except one thing: it cannot show grace. In my opinion, Christians are not doing a very good job of dispensing grace to the world, and we stumble especially in this field of faith and politics.

I know how easy it is to get swept away by the politics of polarization, to shout across picket lines at the "enemy" on the other side. But Jesus commanded, "Love your enemies." Somehow Jesus managed to separate the policy from the person. Anyone, even a half-breed with five husbands or a thief nailed to a cross, was welcome to join his kingdom. The person was more important than any category or label. For Will Campbell, that meant the redneck Kluxers who killed his friend. For Martin Luther King Jr., that meant the white sheriffs who sicked their police dogs on him.

Who is *my* enemy? The abortionist? The Hollywood producer polluting our culture? The politician threatening my moral principles? The drug lord ruling my inner city? If my activism, however well-motivated, drives out love, then I have misunderstood Jesus' gospel. I am stuck with law, not the gospel of grace.

My second conclusion may appear to contradict the first: commitment to a style of grace does not mean Christians will live in perfect harmony with the government. As Kenneth Kaunda, the former President of Zambia, has written, "what a nation needs more than anything else is not a Christian ruler in the palace but a Christian prophet within earshot."

For all its flaws the church at times has, fitfully and imperfectly to be sure, dispensed Jesus' message of grace to the world. It was Christianity, and only Christianity, that brought an end to slavery, and Christianity that inspired the first hospitals and hospices to treat the sick. The same energy drove the early labor movement, women's suffrage, prohibition, human rights campaigns, and civil rights.

To be effective, "gracious" Christians must be wise in the issues they choose to support or oppose. Historically, Christians have tended to go off on tangents. Yes, we have led the way in abolition and civil rights. But Protestants have also veered off on frenzied campaigns against Catholics, against immigration, against Freemasons. Much of society's present concern over Christian activism traces back to those ill-conceived campaigns.

What about today? Are we choosing our battles wisely? Obviously, abortion, sexual issues, and the definitions of life and death are issues worthy of our attention. Yet when I read the literature produced by evangelicals in politics I also read about gun rights, abolishing the Department of Education, the NAFTA trade agreements, the Panama Canal treaty, and term limits for Congress. Too often the agenda of conservative religious groups matches line for line the agenda of conservative politics and does not base its priorities on a transcendent source. Like everyone else, evangelicals have a right to present arguments on all the issues, but the moment we present them as part of some "Christian" platform we abandon our moral high ground. If we expect society to take seriously our contribution, then we must show more wisdom in our choices.

My third conclusion about church-state relations is a principle I borrow from G. K. Chesterton: A coziness between church and state is good for the state and bad for the church.

I have warned against the church becoming "moral extermi-
nators" for the world. Actually, the state needs moral extermina-
tors and may welcome them whenever the church obliges.
President Eisenhower told the nation in 1954, "Our government
makes no sense unless it is founded on a deeply-felt religious
faith—and I don't care what it is."

In a civic sense, Eisenhower was right: society needs religion,
and it matters little what kind. The Nation of Islam helps clean
up the ghetto; the Mormon church makes Utah a low-crime, fam-
ily-friendly state. Founders of the United States recognized that a
democracy especially, dependent less on imposed order and more
on the virtue of free citizens, needs a religious foundation.

We dare not, however, forget the last part of Chesterton's
aphorism: while a coziness between church and state may be good
for the state, it is bad for the church. Herein lies the chief danger
to grace: the state, which runs by the rules of ungrace, gradually
drowns out the church's sublime message of grace.

The church works best as a force of resistance, a counterbalance to the consuming power of the state. The cozier it gets with
government, the more watered-down its message becomes. The
gospel itself changes as it devolves into civil religion.

In sum, the state must always water down the absolute qual-
ity of Jesus' commands and turn them into a form of external
morality—precisely the opposite of the gospel of grace. A state
government can shut down stores and theaters on Sunday, but it
cannot compel worship. It can arrest and punish KKK murderers
but cannot cure their hatred, much less teach them love. It can
pass laws making divorce more difficult but cannot force husbands to love their wives and wives their husbands. It can give
subsidies to the poor but cannot force the rich to show them compassion and justice. It can ban adultery but not lust, theft but not
covetousness, cheating but not pride. It can encourage virtue but
not holiness.

The Music of Grace in God's Word

Read together the following passages from the Bible.

Matthew 5:43–47
Galatians 5:16–26

~

The Harmony of Grace Around Me and Within
(25 Minutes)

If you are in a larger group, break into groups of four to six for this discussion time. Introduce yourselves to each other if necessary. Think back on your childhood. Whom did you consider your enemy? Maybe the school bully or a mean neighbor? Tell the group about this person.

1. Growing up, did you go to a public or private school? How much Christian influence was evident in your school? Did you regularly pledge allegiance to the American or Christian flag? Was prayer a part of your school day? Was God discussed openly? Did Christian clubs or organizations meet on campus?

2. As you see our society veering away from God, which of the following Bible characters do you tend to identify with?

- Elijah, who hid in caves and made lightning raids on Ahab's pagan regime. I mostly stay in my Christian community but at times feel compelled to speak out, protest, or warn the secular community.
- Obadiah, who worked within the system, running Ahab's palace while sheltering God's true prophets on the side. I'm very much a part of secular society and feel this gives me knowledge, influence, and the opportunity to support fellow Christians.
- Daniel, who loyally served a heathen empire. I serve faithfully within the secular society yet try to let my Christian values permeate all I do. I hope to never compromise my beliefs to meet secular expectations.
- Jonah, who called down judgment on a heathen empire. I feel an urgency to tell our secular society that it is wrong and will be judged by God if it doesn't repent.
- Esther, who entered into a union with a heathen and through her godly spirit was able to save God's people. I have a lasting tie to an unbeliever and pray that God uses me in this person's life by revealing true faith through me.
- Paul, who appealed his case all the way to Caesar. I will go as far as necessary in the political realm to oppose unbiblical policies, acting respectfully yet passionately.

3. Consider Ralph Reed's statement as he renounces the use of hysteria and character assassination in fighting against the secular world. He says, "If we succeed, it will be because we followed [Martin Luther King Jr.'s] example always to love those who hate us, doing battle 'with Christian weapons and with Christian love.' If we fail, it will not be a failure of money or methods, but a failure of the heart and soul. . . . Every word we say and every action we take should reflect God's grace."

   In what ways have you observed the use of hysteria and character assassination? How does this kind of approach make you feel? How do you feel about Martin Luther King Jr.'s approach?

Look again at the approaches of the Bible characters in question 2. Are all these approaches right options for Christians today? Can King's approach be incorporated into each of these? If so, how?

4. Look at the story (on pages 244–45 in the book) of Mother Teresa when she spoke about abortion at a National Prayer Breakfast. She said that America has become a selfish nation, in danger of losing the proper meaning of love: "giving until it hurts." She understands that sacrificial love is one of the most powerful weapons in the Christian's arsenal of grace.

Do you think it is mainly the secular society that has lost sight of the need for sacrificial love? In what ways have Christians lost sight of this attitude?

In what areas have you had to make a decision of whether or not to love sacrificially? Perhaps in areas such as giving money; caring for the poor, sick, or homeless; parenting

a special-needs or prodigal child; loving an ornery neighbor; or caring for foster children?

5. How does a Christian go about choosing battles wisely?
For instance, how do we discern whether issues like
euthanasia, gun rights, or the capital gains tax are closely
related to biblical imperatives and therefore should be tied
to a Christian platform?

6. I have commented that the state, which runs by the rules
of ungrace, gradually drowns out the church's sublime
message of grace. The church works best as a force of
resistance, a counterbalance to the consuming power of
the state.

Do you agree? How do these thoughts fit with your
view of the separation of church and state? As you think
and pray about these issues, do you feel God revealing to
you the *power* of grace? Does grace still feel at times like
a risky forfeiture of power? Do you sometimes feel one
way in your mind but another way in your heart?

Do you have any prayer needs to share with the others?

God's Song of Grace to Me
(10–15 Minutes)

Listen to some music about grace together. Then spend some time being quiet together before God. You may want to meditate on Jesus' words about love printed below. Or you may want to write a prayer or record your thoughts on this session. Write in your journal or use the space provided.

Grace Notes

Listen together to the song "Your Love Broke Through" by Keith Green. Find a recording of the song by Keith Green, or you can find the song sung by Glad on the CD or cassette titled *The Acapella Project III* (Light, 1996). If you are not able to locate Keith Green's song, find a hymnal and sing together the song "More Like the Master." Sing along with a guitar, piano, or *a capella*.

You have heard that it was said, "Love your neighbor and hate your enemy." But I tell you: Love your enemies and pray for those who persecute you, that you may be sons of your Father in heaven. He causes his sun to rise on the evil and the good, and sends rain on the righteous and the unrighteous. If you love those who love you, what reward will you get? Are not even the tax collectors doing that?

Matthew 5:43–46

Joining in the Song of Grace

- Commit to pray this week for those who anger you, whether they be family, personal acquaintances, or a group or individual you know from afar. Pray blessing upon these people. Pray for God's fervent, merciful love to have a profound effect on their lives.

- Consider making a pledge to follow eight principles set forth by Martin Luther King Jr.'s organization. You may want to pledge to follow these principles for the coming week or maybe for the coming month or year.

1. Meditate daily on the teachings and life of Jesus.
2. Remember always that the . . . movement . . . seeks justice and reconciliation, not victory.
3. Walk and talk in the manner of love, for God is love.
4. Pray daily to be used by God in order that all people might be free.
5. Sacrifice personal wishes in order that all people might be free.
6. Observe with both friend and foe the ordinary rules of courtesy.
7. Seek to perform regular service for others and for the world.
8. Refrain from violence of fist, tongue, or heart.

Background Music of Grace This Week
(Optional)

Read the following Bible passages this week in your quiet moments. Reflect on these readings as your time allows.

Day 1: Matthew 7:1–6
Day 2: John 15:1–17
Day 3: John 15:18–16:4
Day 4: 1 John 1:5–2:14
Day 5: 1 John 4:7–21

Patches of Green

Chapter 19

Long after a society begins to decay, signs of its former life continue to assert themselves. Without knowing why, people cling to moral customs of the past, the "habits of the heart" in Robert Bellah's phrase.

Consider Russia. The communist government attacked Russia's heritage with an anti-religious fury unprecedented in human history. They razed churches, mosques, and synagogues, banned religious instruction to children, shuttered seminaries and monasteries, imprisoned and killed priests. We all know what happened, of course. After tens of millions of deaths and after experiencing social and moral chaos, the Russian people finally awoke.

When I visited Russia in 1991, I saw a people starved for grace. The economy, indeed the entire society, was in a state of free fall, and everyone had someone to blame. I noted that ordinary Russian citizens had the demeanor of battered children: lowered heads, halting speech, eyes darting this way and that. Whom could they trust? Just as a battered child finds it hard to believe in order and love, these people were finding it hard to believe in a God who sovereignly controls the universe and who passionately loves them. They find it hard to believe in grace. Yet without grace, what will end the cycle of ungrace in Russia?

I left Russia overwhelmed at the necessary changes ahead of them, and yet I also left with a sense of grim hope. To use Jesus' metaphor, I saw the preservative effect of a sprinkling of salt on a whole society.

I heard from ordinary citizens who now relished their freedom to worship. Most had learned about the faith from a
babushka, an old grandmother. When the state cracked down on
the church, it ignored this group: let the old women sweep the
floors and sell the candles and cling to the traditions until they all
die off, they reasoned. The aged hands of the *babushki,* though,
rocked the cradles. Young churchgoers today often say they first
learned about God in childhood through the hymns and stories
Grandma would whisper as they drifted off to sleep.

On the long airplane flight from Moscow to Chicago, I had
much time to reflect on what I had seen in Russia. While there, I
felt like Alice in Wonderland. The government was investing bil-
lions of rubles to help restore churches damaged or destroyed by the
Communist regime. We prayed with the Supreme Soviet and with
the KGB. We saw Bibles for sale in the Russian government buildings. The editors of *Pravda* asked if one of us could write a religious
column for the front page of their newspaper. Educators invited us
to submit a curriculum based on the Ten Commandments.

I had the distinct impression that God was moving—not in the
spiritualized sense of that phrase but quite literally packing up and
moving. Western Europe now pays God little heed, the United States
is pushing God to the margins, and perhaps the future of God's kingdom belongs to places like Korea, China, Africa, and Russia. The
kingdom of God thrives where its subjects follow the desires of the
King—does that describe the United States of America today?

I must admit that my return to the United States gave me little reason to hope that Russia and the world might learn grace
from Christians here. Christians seemed more interested in power
than in grace.

Jesus' images portray the kingdom as a kind of secret force.
Sheep among wolves, treasure hidden in a field, the tiniest seed in
the garden, wheat growing among weeds, a pinch of yeast worked
into bread dough, a sprinkling of salt on meat—all these hint at
a movement that works within society, changing it from the inside
out. You do not need a shovelful of salt to preserve a slab of ham;
a dusting will suffice.

Jesus did not leave an organized host of followers, for he knew that a handful of salt would gradually work its way through the mightiest empire in the world. Against all odds, the great institutions of Rome—the law code, libraries, the Senate, Roman legions, roads, aqueducts, public monuments—gradually crumbled, but the little band to whom Jesus gave these images prevailed and continues on today.

Christians today also live by a different set of rules. We are a "peculiar" people, wrote Bonhoeffer, which he defined as extraordinary, unusual, that which is not a matter of course. Jesus was not crucified for being a good citizen, for being just a little nicer than everyone else. The powers of his day correctly saw him and his followers as subversives because they took orders from a higher power than Rome or Jerusalem.

What would a subversive church look like in the modern United States? Surely a peculiar people should demonstrate a higher standard of personal ethics than the surrounding world. Yet, to take just one example, pollster George Barna discovered that born-again Christians in modern America actually have a higher rate of divorce (twenty-seven percent) than nonbelievers (twenty-three percent); those who describe themselves as funda mentalists have the highest percentage of all (thirty percent). Indeed, four of the six states with the highest divorce rates fall in the region known as the Bible Belt. Far from being peculiar, modern Christians tend to look just like everyone else, only more so. Unless our personal ethics rise above the level around us, we can hardly hope to act as a moral preservative.

Even if Christians demonstrated the highest standard of ethics, however, that alone would not fulfill the gospel. After all, the Pharisees had impeccable ethics. Rather, Jesus reduced the mark of a Christian to one word. "By this all men will know that you are my disciples," he said: "if you *love* one another." The most subversive act the church can take is consistently to obey that one command.

Perhaps the reason politics has proved such a snare for the church is that power rarely coexists with love. People in power draw up lists of friends and enemies, then reward their friends and punish their enemies. Christians are commanded to love even their enemies. Chuck Colson, who perfected the art of power politics under the Nixon Administration, now says he has little faith in politics to solve the social problems of today. Our best efforts at changing society will fall short unless the church can teach the world how to love.

During the Brezhnev era at the height of the Cold War, Billy Graham visited Russia and met with government and church leaders. Conservatives back home reproached him for treating the Russians with such courtesy and respect. He should have taken a more prophetic role, they said, by condemning the abuses of human rights and religious liberty. One of his critics accused him of setting the church back fifty years. Graham listened, lowered his head, and replied, "I am deeply ashamed. I have been trying very hard to set the church back two thousand years."

Politics draws lines between people; in contrast, Jesus' love cuts across those lines and dispenses grace. That does not mean, of course, that Christians should not involve themselves in politics. It simply means that as we do so we must not let the rules of power displace the command to love.

The Christian knows to serve the weak not because they deserve it but because God extended his love to us when we deserved the opposite. Christ came *down* from heaven, and whenever his disciples entertained dreams of prestige and power he reminded them that the greatest is the one who serves. The ladder of power reaches up, the ladder of grace reaches down.

As a journalist, I have had the privilege of seeing many wonderful examples of Christians who dispense grace. Unlike political activists, this group does not often make the newspapers. Faithfully they serve, seasoning our culture with the preservative of the gospel. I tremble to imagine what the modern United States would look like without the "salt of the earth" in its midst.

Rousseau said the church set up an irresolvable loyalty dilemma. How can Christians be good citizens of this world if they are primarily concerned about the next world? The people I mention at the end of chapter 19 disprove his argument. As C. S.

Lewis has noted, those most conscious of another world have made the most effective Christians in this one.

The Music of Grace in God's Word

Read together the following passages from the Bible.

Matthew 13:31–33, 44–46

The Harmony of Grace Around Me and Within
(20 Minutes)

If you are in a larger group, break into groups of four to six for this discussion time. Introduce yourselves to each other if necessary. Tell the others about something you once found. Maybe a piece of jewelry or a large bill. What did you do with what you'd found?

1. Review the paragraphs about the Soviet Union on pages 255–57 in the book. How did the gospel survive seventy years of Communism and persecution? Do you see any kind of spiritual revival similar to that in Russia occurring in our society? If so, what has brought about the revival?

   How do you feel about my impression that God is "packing up and moving" to places like Korea, China, Africa, and Russia?

2. I tell of my experience on a panel discussing "culture wars." If you were on such a panel, maybe at your church or at a nearby civic center, what statement would you make in voicing your own analysis or opinion? Do the culture wars require Christians to launch an offensive? Strengthen our defense? If so, what should these actions look like?

3. Look at the parables you read earlier from Matthew 13. How do these parables speak to the previous question about the culture wars? (See also the two paragraphs in the summary, beginning, "Jesus' images portray . . .") Jesus spoke in metaphors. How should his message actually play itself out in modern, democratic society?

4. On pages 261–62 in the book look at the paragraphs on the dissidents in Eastern Europe, who finally refused to act in fear and began instead speaking freely and telling the truth. What would it look like if Christians used that same approach in secular society? In what ways is your church or group of Christian friends doing this, rather than simply reflecting back the image of the society around it?

Think about this question in light of the paragraph on page 262 in the book beginning, "If the world despises a notorious sinner . . ." and in light of the quote by Ron Sider on page 265. How well does your church stack up when compared with the church described in these paragraphs?

5. Look at the story (on page 265 in the book) of my friend who worked at a pregnancy counseling center. She offered coffee and doughnuts to pro-choice demonstrators outside her center on a cold morning. Are you someone who occasionally offers "random acts of grace" like this? Be honest. Some of us are more impulsive than others. Some of us often feel a desire to love like this but don't often follow through. What is typical of you?

6. I have mentioned organizations and individuals whom I've come to know as a journalist. Those such as Habitat for Humanity and Chuck Colson, among others, have become examples to me of dispensing grace. Often we encounter people close to home who share grace in small, quiet ways. Who comes to mind when you consider Christians who dispense grace? Do you know people who, in Robert Bellah's words, "cherish the vision of a just and gentle world"? Maybe a personal friend or family member comes to mind. Maybe someone you have read about or watched from a distance has modeled faithful, mercy-filled service.

Do you have any prayer needs to express to the group?

Of one hundred men, one will read the Bible; the ninety-nine will read the Christian.

Dwight L. Moody

God's Song of Grace to Me
(10–15 Minutes)

Listen to some music about grace together, and then spend some time in silence with God. Let the music be the beginning of a time of prayer and surrender of yourself to God. If you choose to write a prayer, you can use the space provided or write in your journal.

Grace Notes

Listen together to the song "Any Road, Any Cost" by Point of Grace. It is found on their CD or cassette titled *life love and other mysteries* (Word, 1996). The song is a prayer of surrender, telling God we will follow him down any road at any cost, doing what his love compels us to do. Make an effort to obtain this CD or cassette for this session. The song is powerful and will help the group in committing together to follow as God leads.

Joining in the Song of Grace

- This week pray that God would move you to offer a "random act of grace" toward another whom you might not naturally be inclined to love. You might enact this gesture of love this week, or you might just begin praying for God's leading toward an act you will commit later on.
- Stop at a library or bookstore this week and choose a biography to begin reading. Find a true story of someone who committed himself or herself to loving, selfless service of others.
- Consider gathering together with your group to watch the video *Amazing Grace with Bill Moyers,* if you have not already done so. Information for ordering or renting this video is found in the introduction to this study guide.

Background Music of Grace This Week
(Optional)

Read the following Bible passages this week in your quiet moments. Reflect on these readings as your time allows.

Day 1: 1 Corinthians 13:1–13
Day 2: 2 Corinthians 4:1–18
Day 3: 2 Corinthians 5:11–21
Day 4: Ephesians 4:17–5:21
Day 5: Ephesians 3:14–21

~

Brennan Manning writes of a time he and his wife were roaming the French Quarter of New Orleans. A young girl with a radiant smile approached, introduced herself, and pinned a flower on both of them. Then she asked if they would like to make a donation to her mission, the Unification Church. "Your founder is

Doctor Sun Myung Moon, so I guess that means you're a Moonie?" Manning asked. She said yes and hung her head.

To her surprise Manning gave this response. "You know something, Susan? I deeply admire your integrity and your fidelity to your conscience. You're out here tramping the streets doing what you really believe in. You are a challenge to anyone who claims the name 'Christian.'" He and his wife both hugged the startled flower peddler.

"Are you Christians?" the girl asked. When they replied yes, she paused for a moment to get control of her emotions. Then she said, "I've been on my mission here in the Quarter for eight days now. You're the first Christians who have ever been nice to me. The others have either looked at me with contempt or screamed and told me that I was possessed by a demon. One woman hit me with her Bible."[1]

Gravity and Grace

Chapter 20

~

Karl Barth made the comment that Jesus' gift of forgiveness, of grace, was to him more astonishing than Jesus' miracles. Miracles broke the physical laws of the universe; forgiveness broke the moral rules. "The beginning of good is perceived in the midst of bad. . . . The simplicity and comprehensiveness of grace—who shall measure it?"

Who shall measure it indeed? I have merely walked the perimeter of grace, as one walks around a cathedral far too large and grand to behold at one glance. Having begun with questions—What's so amazing about grace and why don't Christians show more of it?—I now end with a final question: What does a grace-full Christian look like?

Perhaps I should rephrase the question, How does a grace-full Christian *look?* The Christian life, I believe, does not primarily center on ethics or rules but rather involves a new way of seeing. I escape the force of spiritual "gravity" when I begin to see myself as a sinner who cannot please God by any method of self-improvement or self-enlargement. Only then can I turn to God for outside help—for grace—and to my amazement I learn that a holy God already loves me despite my defects. I escape the force of gravity again when I recognize my neighbors also as sinners, loved by God. A grace-full Christian is one who looks at the world through "grace-tinted lenses."

As a child, I put on my best behavior on Sunday mornings, dressing up for God and for the Christians around me. It never occurred to me that church was a place to be honest. Now, though, as I seek to look at the world through the lens of grace, I realize that imperfection is the prerequisite for grace. Light only gets in through the cracks.

Once my view of myself changed, I began to see the church in a different light too: as a community of people thirsty for grace. Like alcoholics on the path to recovery, we share a mutually acknowledged weakness.

I think back one more time to the prostitute's comment at the beginning of this book: "Church! Why would I ever go there? I was already feeling terrible about myself. They would just make me feel worse." Church should be a haven for people who feel terrible about themselves—theologically, that is our ticket for entry. God needs humble people (which usually means humbled people) to accomplish his work. Whatever makes us feel superior to other people, whatever tempts us to convey a sense of superiority, that is gravity, not grace.

I marvel at Jesus' tenderness in dealing with people who expressed longings for grace. For example, John gives the account of Jesus' impromptu conversation with a woman at a well. In those days the husband initiated divorce: this Samaritan woman had been dumped by five different men. Jesus could have begun by pointing out what a mess the woman had made of her life. Yet he did not say, "Young woman, do you realize what an immoral thing you're doing, living with a man who is not your husband?" Rather he said, in effect, *I sense you are very thirsty.* Jesus went on to tell her that the water she was drinking would never satisfy and then offered her living water to quench her thirst forever.

I try to recall this spirit of Jesus when I encounter someone of whom I morally disapprove. *This must be a very thirsty person,* I tell myself. I once talked with the priest Henri Nouwen just after he had returned from San Francisco. He had visited various ministries to AIDS victims and was moved with compassion by their sad stories. "They want love so bad, it's literally killing them," he said. He saw them as thirsty people panting after the wrong kind of water.

When I am tempted to recoil in horror from sinners, from "different" people, I remember what it must have been like for

Jesus to live on earth. Perfect, sinless, Jesus had every right to be repulsed by the behavior of those around him. Yet he treated notorious sinners with mercy and not judgment.

One who has been touched by grace will no longer look on those who stray as "those evil people" or "those poor people who need our help." Nor must we search for signs of "loveworthiness." Grace teaches us that God loves because of who God is, not because of who we are. Categories of worthiness do not apply.

Christianity has a principle, "Hate the sin but love the sinner," which is more easily preached than practiced. If Christians could simply recover that practice, modeled so exquisitely by Jesus, we would go a long way toward fulfilling our calling as dispensers of God's grace.

Christians should not compromise in hating sin, says C. S. Lewis. Rather we should hate the sins in others in the same way we hate them in ourselves: being sorry the person has done such things and hoping that somehow, sometime, somewhere, that person will be cured.

Bill Moyers' documentary film on the hymn "Amazing Grace" includes a scene filmed in Wembley Stadium in London. Various musical groups, mostly rock bands, had gathered together in celebration of the changes in South Africa, and for some reason the promoters scheduled an opera singer, Jessye Norman, as the closing act.

The film cuts back and forth between scenes of the unruly crowd in the stadium and Jessye Norman being interviewed. For twelve hours groups like Guns 'n' Roses have blasted the crowd through banks of speakers, riling up fans already high on booze and dope. The crowd yells for more curtain calls, and the rock groups oblige. Meanwhile, Jessye Norman sits in her dressing room discussing "Amazing Grace" with Moyers.

The hymn was written, of course, by John Newton, a coarse, cruel slave trader. Even after his conversion, he continued to ply his trade. Later, though, he renounced his profession and joined William Wilberforce in the fight against slavery. John Newton never lost sight of the depths from which he had been lifted. He never lost sight of grace. When he wrote " . . . That saved a wretch like me," he meant those words with all his heart.

In the film, Jessye Norman tells Bill Moyers that Newton may have written the words to fit an old tune sung by the slaves themselves. He redeemed the song, just as he had been redeemed.

Finally, the time comes for her to sing. A single circle of light follows Norman, a majestic African-American woman wearing a flowing African dashiki, as she strolls onstage. No backup band, no musical instruments, just Jessye. The crowd stirs, restless. Few recognize the opera diva. A voice yells for more Guns 'n' Roses. Others take up the cry. The scene is getting ugly.

Alone, *a capella,* Jessye Norman begins to sing, very slowly:

Amazing grace, how sweet the sound
    That saved a wretch like me!
I once was lost but now am found—
    Was blind, but now I see.

A remarkable thing happens in Wembley Stadium that night. Seventy thousand raucous fans fall silent before her aria of grace.

By the time Norman reaches the second verse, "'Twas grace that taught my heart to fear, And grace my fears relieved . . . ," the soprano has the crowd in her hands.

By the time she reaches the third verse, "'Tis grace has brought me safe this far, And grace will lead me home," several thousand fans are singing along, digging far back in nearly lost memories for words they heard long ago.

Jessye Norman later confessed she had no idea what power descended on Wembley Stadium that night. I think I know. The world thirsts for grace. When grace descends, the world falls silent before it.

The Music of Grace in God's Word

Read together the following passages from the Bible.

Matthew 7:15–23
Luke 7:36–50

The Harmony of Grace Around Me and Within
(25 Minutes)

If you are in a larger group, break into groups of four to six for this discussion time. Introduce yourselves to one another if necessary. Can you recall an embarrassing moment when you thought you knew someone but in reality the person was a stranger? Or vice versa—when you didn't recognize someone you should have known? Tell the group about your embarrassing moment.

1. Reflect on your life with God in the past. Have you worn masks in front of God or others? Do any of the following speak of where you've been with God in the past or where you could be now?

   - I have worn the mask of ultraspirituality. I've got a lot of head knowledge, and others have respected my spiritual leadership. It's easier to help the needy than it is to reveal my own neediness.
   - I have worn the mask of professed purity. I've prided myself on doing it all right and have considered myself an example for others to follow. After walking with that mask for a while, it's difficult to let on about the weaknesses that plague me.
   - I have worn the mask of miracle worker. At some point my fervency for serving others grew into a sort of savior complex. I've had a hard time letting others struggle, and worse, I haven't let myself struggle.
   - I have worn the mask of self-proclaimed prophet. I've taken it upon myself to warn others of God's judgment. I've been so busy trying to force God upon others that I've forced him right out of my own life.

   "We cannot find Him unless we know we need Him," wrote Thomas Merton. Can you pinpoint any experience or circumstance in your life that revealed to you your deep need for God? Are you still in tune with that neediness today?

2. In the book on pages 275–77 look at the paragraphs in which I describe the Alcoholics Anonymous group that met in my church basement. Alcoholics Anonymous runs on two principles: radical honesty and radical dependence. Have you ever been part of a group that lived out these principles, a group in which nobody fooled anybody else and members who were all at the same level of brokenness shared true love? Tell the others about your experience.

3. Consider the individuals I describe on pages 277–78 in the book as I talk about assisting with church communion. Mabel, a senior citizen who had once been a prostitute. Gus and Mildred, newly married seniors living near poverty but in marital bliss. Adolphus, an angry young black man who made occasional violent outbursts while at church. Christina and Reiner, a German couple who feared for their son's safety as he began a mission trip to India. As you look around your church during a worship service, how much do you know of the lives of those around you? Do you find that the better you get to know others, the more vulnerable you are able to be in your church community? Why is that? What keeps us from being more vulnerable with each other?

Can you think of a scene in which someone truly did express need?

4. Douglas Coupland, who coined the term "Generation X," concluded in his book *Life after God,* "My secret is that I need God—that I am sick and can no longer make it alone. I need God to help me give, because I no longer seem capable of kindness; to help me love, as I seem beyond being able to love." Jesus looked at those like Coupland, whom the world saw only as sinful, and said in effect, "I sense you are very thirsty." What groups of people do you tend to view as "sinners"? In what ways are they probably thirsty?

5. Take a few minutes to reflect on your study of grace during the last fourteen weeks. What one or two things did God impress on you most strongly during your study? Are there issues you are still grappling with? What have you appreciated about your time with the group?

Do you have any prayer requests to share with the group for the weeks ahead?

God's Song of Grace to Me
(10–15 Minutes)

Listen together to the song "Amazing Grace." Then instead of spending this time in silent prayer or meditation, stay in your groups of four to six and pray together. You may want to hold hands or lay hands on one another. Pray spontaneously, or take turns praying for the special needs of each person, with the group laying hands on that person as he or she is prayed for. End your prayer for each person with the blessing, "Grace to you."

Grace Notes

Conclude this course by listening together to the song "Amazing Grace." If you have a copy of the Bill Moyers documentary on the hymn "Amazing Grace," you may want to arrange to have a television and VCR available for this prayer time. (Some larger video rental stores have this video available for rent.) Play the scene in which Jessye Norman enters the stage and sings "Amazing Grace." If you haven't obtained this video, you can locate an audio recording of Jessye Norman singing "Amazing Grace." This is found on her CD or cassette titled *Amazing Grace* (Philips, 1991). It is available in many mainstream music stores. If you cannot obtain either of these, you can use Helen Baylor's version of the song or any other version. Or sing the hymn together.

Joining in the Song of Grace

- Pay attention this week to your reactions toward people in the news or those you meet who are acting in unchristian ways. What are your initial feelings toward them? Does love and compassion accompany your anger or dislike? Pray that God would guide your responses.
- Spend some time this week looking back through this study guide and your book. Review those ideas that impacted you, and recall the ways God has spoken to you. Read through your notes and journal entries. Spend some time in prayer, asking God to continue the work of grace he has begun in you.

Background Music of Grace This Week
(Optional)

Read the following Bible passages and reading this week in your quiet moments as you reflect on God's grace. Use these readings as your time allows.

Day 1: Colossians 2:6–23
Day 2: Colossians 3:1–17
Day 3: Colossians 4:2–6
Day 4: 1 Timothy 2:1–8
Day 5: Titus 3:1–11

Notes

Week One: The Last Best Word

1. Dean Merrill, *Sinners in the Hands of an Angry Church* (Grand Rapids: Zondervan, 1997), ch. 5. Original source: Tony Campolo, *The Kingdom of God Is a Party* (Dallas: Word, 1990), 3–9.

Week Two: What Grace Is and Isn't

1. Bill Hybels and Mark Mittelberg, *Becoming a Contagious Christian* (Grand Rapids: Zondervan, 1994), 54–55.

2. Patrick Kavanaugh, *The Spiritual Lives of Great Composers* (Nashville: Sparrow, 1992), 11–16.

Week Three: Grace in the Bible

1. Ibid., 27–33.

Week Four: Forgiveness: An Unnatural Act

1. Michelle Mahoney, "Racial Forgiveness," *Denver Post* (June 4, 1996), 1E.

Week Five: Why Forgive?

1. Kavanaugh, *The Spiritual Lives of Great Composers,* 51–56.

2. Patricia Raybon, *My First White Friend* (New York: Viking Penguin, 1996), 224–26.

Week Six: Getting Even

1. Simon Wiesenthal, *The Sunflower* (New York: Schocken, 1976).

2. Gary Smith, "What Makes Jimmy Run?" *Life* (November 1995), 108.

Week Thirteen: Patches of Green

1. Brennan Manning, *Abba's Child* (Colorado Springs: NavPress, 1994), 77.